WILD
Weekends

CLAIRE KEETON
MARIANNE SCHWANKHART

WILD
Weekends

PLACES TO GO
Things to do

BOOK**STORM**

MACMILLAN

CONTENTS

WEEKENDS

4

ACKNOWLEDGEMENTS

The concept for an adventure-travel column for the *Sunday Times Travel Weekly* supplement came from our editors and managers. We are indebted to them for thinking it up, funding it and approving our trips. We know how privileged we are to have this job.

To the *Sunday Times* travel team – editor Andrew Unsworth, deputy editor Paul Ash, subeditor Elizabeth Sleith (whose headlines are reprinted in this book) and designer Vernice Shaw – a special thanks for their support and patience every week, and to logistics wizard Sandy Hattingh for pulling off amazing feats.

Bookstorm publisher, Louise Grantham, is the force behind this book. We are grateful for her enthusiasm in its conceptualisation and for taking a risk on it.

Without the invaluable support of editorial project manager Russell Clarke and Mark Ronan editing our copy, the book would not have taken shape so smoothly. We appreciate their contribution.

From Claire
I would like to thank my extraordinary and lovely son, Zade, now seven years old, for exploring the country with me and tolerating my absences. I appreciate the commitment of his father, Ernest, for sharing the parenting every step of the way and enabling me to travel regularly. Thanks also to my climbing friends for child support at the crags from the time my son was a baby. This has allowed me to climb and travel with Zade from Montagu to Norway. Finally, we are grateful to the Mountain Club of South Africa, to which we belong, for conserving the Magaliesberg kloofs, where we spend most weekends.

From Marianne
To Oliver, my husband, who has never given me a hard time about my travels and adventures but instead always supports my ideas. I often come home in torn clothes, looking wild and scraggly, to someone keen to share my happiness.

Declaration
The authors stayed as non-paying guests at the following establishments: Welgevonden Game Reserve, Waterberg; Rhino Walking Safaris, Kruger National Park; Kosi Forest Lodge, Kosi Bay; Cedar Peak, Groot Winterhoek; Prana Lodge, Chintsa; Tsala Treetop Lodge and Tamodi Lodge, Garden Route; and AfriSki, Lesotho.

INTRODUCTION

Between us we had explored 58 countries for more than 20 years, climbing big mountains and walls, rafting rivers and camping in remote places, including in South Africa, when our editors at the *Sunday Times* approached us with a dream job offer: Claire researching and writing, and Marianne photographing adventure travel for *Travel Weekly*.

We're in our element outdoors, and travelling is easy because we've been friends for a long time – good enough friends to share a toothbrush in the desert and be stuck together in roadworks for hours. We did our first trip together 10 years ago when we hardly knew each other, travelling around five countries in southern Africa in Claire's old Suzuki, reporting on famine and HIV during the day, and driving and camping at night.

About a year into the job, we were again approached, this time by Bookstorm publishers, with another dream project: to compile our experiences into a travel book. From the initial discussion, the idea developed rapidly into this book, which gives us a chance to share our experiences of great places to visit and ways to unwind.

Working as the Girls Gone Wild team, we have been lucky to travel around South Africa and neighbouring countries for the *Sunday Times* since July 2011. *Wild Weekends* is a guide to the places and activities we would recommend from our trips. This collection describes places we chose to visit and others to which we were invited and would go back if we could.

Claire's son has joined us on the road for regular trips for work and in our free time. *Wild Weekends* shows that it is possible to experience adventures with young children, whether it's canopy gliding above waterfalls or canoeing on a lagoon. We hope readers will take ideas from this book and discover new frontiers to share with us.

Go wild!

Claire and Marianne

MAP OF SOUTHERN AFRICA

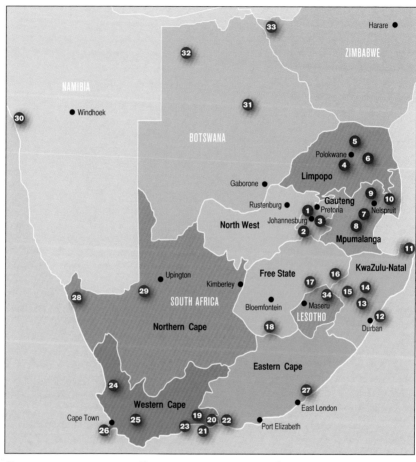

1. Magaliesberg
2. Carletonville
3. Johannesburg
4. Waterberg
5. Soutpansberg
6. Magoebaskloof
7. Kaapsehoop
8. Waterval Boven
9. White River
10. Kruger National Park
11. Kosi Bay
12. Durban
13. Howick & Karkloof Waterfalls
14. Tugela River
15. The Drakensberg
16. Harrismith
17. Clarens & Ficksburg
18. Gariep Dam & Smithfield
19. Prince Albert & Oudtshoorn
20. Four rivers: Keurbooms, Kruis,
    Storms & Bloukrans
21. Plettenberg Bay
22. Greater Tsitsikamma
23. Mossel Bay
24. Cederberg & Groot Winterhoek
25. Montagu & Simonskloof
26. Cape Town
27. Chintsa, Glengarriff & Morgans Bay
28. Richtersveld
29. Orange River & Green Kalahari
30. Namibia: Spitzkoppe & Swakopmund
31. Botswana: Makgadikgadi Pans
    & Central Kalahari
32. Botswana: Okavango Delta
33. Zimbabwe: Zambezi River & Vic Falls
34. Lesotho: AfriSki

HOW TO USE THIS BOOK

This book is divided into two sections – Weekends and Activities.

The **Weekends** section describes the places to go and things to do that we recommend from our travels in the last 18 months. Most destinations are easily accessible for a weekend away from one or another of South Africa's cities – but there's a wild weekend to suit everyone, no matter the depth of your pocket or where in the country you live.

Claire wrote most of this section (except for the Richtersveld, penned by Marianne) and so most of the opinions expressed here are Claire's.

The **Activities** section introduces you to all the weird and wonderful leisure pursuits we have undertaken during these weekends away. Some activities are more demanding than others, so we have included our comments and thoughts on each activity, the places we think are most enjoyable for specific activities, as well as useful hints and tips, and information and resources. Marianne wrote most of this section except for scuba diving, snorkelling and shark diving, and we jointly penned ocean sports.

We have undertaken loads of activities, so we've have grouped them by their base element (ocean, bush, adrenalin, and so on) and given each a logo. You can quickly see which activities might interest you by glancing at the logos at the beginning of each chapter.

PRICING GUIDE

We have created a general pricing guide for the activities and places to stay, using six colour-coded categories, so you can figure out what your budget will allow:

- Under R150 per person
- Between R150 and R300 per person
- Between R300 and R500 per person
- Between R500 and R800 per person
- Between R800 and R1 500 per person
- Over R1 500 per person

We decided to create a generic cost guide because prices change constantly, and the last thing we want is an angry Wild Weekender to chase us down because the price of canoe hire in East London has changed! Our advice is to confirm the exact pricing when booking your trip or activity.

WEEKENDS

MAGALIESBERG: SOUL SANCTUARY

1

The Magaliesberg mountain range, where I hike and climb most weekends with Marianne, friends and my son, remains as wonderful to me now as when I first discovered these kloofs nearly 20 years ago. I once took a year off work (not, strictly speaking, a sabbatical) to go rock climbing around the world with a friend, and after coming home we appreciated the seclusion, high rock walls, pools and wildlife of the Magaliesberg even more.

In South Africa, we are lucky to have vast tracts of wilderness like the Magaliesberg, where it's possible to be the only person boulder hopping down a tranquil gorge. The Magaliesberg ridge, which runs from Pretoria in the east to Rustenburg in the west, has kloofs on its southern and northern slopes, and and the rock dates back about 2 billion years.

Climbing its ochre sandstone, in the stillness with the sun on your back, while eagles soar, is exhilarating. Resting on a ledge halfway up a climbing route, with the river far below, is the ultimate peaceful experience. When Marianne and I went hiking in Mountain Sanctuary Park on a weekday, we came across baboons, duikers and eagles – but not a single person. During weekends and holidays, however, this privately owned nature reserve gets booked out with visitors from the nearby towns of Pretoria, Rustenburg and Joburg. (Find out more about rock climbing on page 178.)

MOUNTAIN SANCTUARY PARK

The publicly accessible areas of the Magaliesberg, such as Mountain Sanctuary Park and Fernkloof, are mostly on the north-facing side of the range. The Magaliesberg has many resorts, lodges, guest farms and game reserves where people can hike, climb, horse ride and go on game rides – which are found along a route called the Magalies Meander.

Mountain Sanctuary, which was voted among the 2012 top-10 nature reserves in the country, is deservedly one of the most popular. At more than 1 000 hectares, it is the largest privately owned nature reserve here, and guests are allowed to walk where they want, unlike many other places. The owner, Owen Sutton, who has a passion for conservation, explains that this allows guests freedom to explore, and dramatically reduces impact on the mountain, which is a very sensitive habitat. Visitors can swim in all the mountain pools and streams, with the exception of the Grotto.

The park has three hikes and a mountain-bike trail, which forms part of the Magalies Monster race.

TRAILS

The short trails lead to the Slide Pools, the Grotto and the West Pools. Children, and adults unaccustomed to hiking, will enjoy these trails. A rocky path from the rest camp leads to a sign pointing to the Slide Pools, and from there a path winds down to a river that flows over rocks into the pools.

The pools are safe for children to splash and swim in, and adults can use them as plunge pools. The Jacuzzi Pool is about 1.5 metres deep and is big enough for a few adults. The West Pools are great for swimming and, if you go upriver from the shallow rapids at the northern end, you reach the Fountain Pools. The Grotto, a cave with tree roots and a waterfall flowing through it, is cool and you almost expect to catch a glimpse of fairies in the dripping moss and shadows.

PRISTINE KLOOFS

Bordering Mountain Sanctuary Park are four kloofs controlled by the Mountain Club of South Africa:

Cedarberg, Lower Tonquani, Boulder and Upper Tonquani. Permits are required to access these areas and patrols enforce this rule. Like the Mountain Sanctuary reserve, the Mountain Club is committed to looking after the veld and is strict about pollution, particularly in the rivers (the water is clean enough to drink).

Guidelines on conduct, such as staying away from nesting eagles, have been put in place to protect the wildlife. One of my friends has seen a leopard drinking at a pool in Cedarberg Kloof, and Marianne and I spotted a puff adder in Boulder Kloof. Vervet monkeys and baboons abound, and have taunted us (stolen naartjie in one paw) with their climbing prowess, of which we can only dream.

The rock climbing in the Mountain Club kloofs is excellent, with hard sandstone walls up to 150 metres high. Hanging by my fingertips trying to follow Marianne – or any of my more hard-core climbing friends – along a steep roof, or leading a route myself,

is demanding but at the same time relaxing.

Climbing clears your head and the impossible becomes possible in an astonishing way. But if you don't like heights, then bouldering – climbing smaller rocks without ropes – is another activity that allows you to try out the techniques of rock climbing without exposing you to high or long routes. The Magaliesberg has hundreds of boulders for children and adults to practise on, but be mindful, as my young son has discovered, that it's harder to climb down than up.

SLEEPING OUT

Mountain Sanctuary has plenty of space, and in its grassy campsite, radios and other sources of noise are banned, making it a tranquil reserve. The campsite has clean ablution facilities, a swimming pool, a deck and a lapa. The pool has a shallow end popular with small children. If you want more luxurious accommodation, you can try The Feathered Nest lodge not too far away. The lodge has four open-plan cottages with verandahs. There are no TVs. Each cottage has king-size beds with diaphanous drapes, outdoor showers, baths for two and fireplaces that encourage staying indoors – despite the attractions of bush walks or sundowners at the open-air bar. The four-poster bed in the sunny Batis Cottage, on the periphery of the lodge, overlooks a waterhole that attracts wildlife and birds in summer. I liked the space and openness of this stylish room.

IF YOU GO

When to go
The Magaliesberg streams flow strongest in summer, which is the rainy season. Winters are cold at night but its blue days are perfect for hiking and climbing, and the stars are brilliant.

Contacts and rates
- For more information, visit www.magaliesburg.co.za
- Mountain Sanctuary Park: vehicle entrance fee ◼; camping per adult per night ◼; chalets ◼; log cabins ◼. Tel 014 534 0114; web www.mountain-sanctuary.co.za
- For hiking and climbing information, visit Mountain Club of South Africa www.mcsa.org.za/jhbjoom
- The Feathered Nest: per person per night, dinner and breakfast included ◼, with specials offered. Tel 083 378 2735; web www.featherednest.co.za
- Go Vertical Mountaineering Adventures offers climbing (NB the authors have not tested guiding with them). Tel 082 731 4696; email info@govertical.co.za for climbing guides

How to get there
Mountain Sanctuary Park and the other nature and game reserves are about 90 minutes' drive from Joburg and Pretoria, and within striking distance of Rustenburg.

② CARLETONVILLE: 'CHUTING THE BREEZE

Skydiving is the ultimate, effortless thrill. The gold-mining town of Carletonville, about 80 kilometres west of Joburg, is famous not only for its mine dumps but also for an array of parachutes floating down through the sky. In *The Bucket List*, a film starring Jack Nicholson and Morgan Freeman, the two men choose skydiving as one of the things they want to do before they die. Don't wait.

THE THRILL

Somersaulting out of a plane into the clouds is pure fun. When I skydived for the first time, on a stormy Sunday, my exhilaration, unexpectedly, was not diluted by fear. The jump happened too fast to get scared. The ground was far away and I was strapped to a licensed tandem instructor with 10 years' experience, so I felt safe.

But I did feel nervous excitement as the plane climbed nearly 3 300 metres into the sky. I told Marianne, who went skydiving as a student years ago, that it seemed like an insane activity. Nevertheless, I relaxed as soon as we exited the plane and were free-falling in the sky – our average speed was 201 kilometres per hour for the first 40 seconds. And once the parachute opened, the descent slowed suddenly to become silent and calm, until the landing.

If you want a once-in-a-lifetime rush and you can afford to go tandem skydiving, then do it: you won't forget it. Or, even better, if you like it, do a skydiving course so you can pull the ripcord yourself.

OPPOSITE AND ABOVE RIGHT: *Claire going for a tandem skydive* PICS: WARREN HITCHCOCK

THE JUMP

Marianne and I went to Skydive Joburg, a club near Carletonville, on a sunny morning and saw skydivers coming in to land, their parachutes bright in the sky, as we approached the drop zone. I was booked to jump at about noon and, on arrival, we met the organiser, Lizette Vermeulen. When she was starting out, Lizette packed thousands of parachutes to earn cash to fund her addiction. She introduced me to her husband, Glen, who was to be my tandem pilot. Glen, who has done nearly 3 000 jumps, says: 'Skydiving is the coolest thing ever. It's the best thing you can do with your clothes on. You can't explain it to someone who has not done it.'

He explained that he would fetch me about 20 minutes before take-off, strap me into my harness and brief me on the jump. While we were waiting, the clouds mounted overhead and we had a brief storm, making me wonder if I'd get to jump that day. Luckily, the rain cleared, I got a blue overall to put on and was strapped into a harness.

The clouds scattered as we walked out to our plane with its shark's teeth painted on its nose. The aircraft was a PAC 750, designed specially for skydiving. When I asked Glen why I didn't have a helmet and he did, he said a helmet wouldn't help much if we crashed; he needed his because it had an altimeter inside it.

Eleven skydivers, including Glen, a cameraman and me, plus Marianne and another passenger, packed ourselves into the plane. Eight of the divers jumped out together in formation at 11 000 feet, rocking the plane as they exited. Then it was my turn. Glen slid the two of us quickly along a bench towards the open door. At the exit, he tipped my head up to the sky, reminded me to

arch my back and then threw us out. He manoeuvred us into a horizontal position and I could hear a roar as we fell. Then Glen pulled the ripcord and deployed the chute, and we slowed down. Everything went quiet and we got into a seated position.

We drifted down for another 10 minutes or so and Glen explained how we would land. I had to lift my legs so they wouldn't get tangled at awkward angles with his when we touched down. We approached the ground fast until he flared the parachute and we braked, gliding in, sitting down, to a smooth landing.

SKYDIVE JOBURG

This skydiving club is like any macho hangout – the pub is popular (of course), but there's also a clubhouse and a canteen that serves food, from breakfasts and hamburgers to

snacks and a home-cooked dinner on Saturday nights. Children play on the lawns, while adults in the bar watch their mates touch down on the drop zone in front, celebrating another safe landing with a beer.

If you want to stay over, there are wooden cabins [●], bunk rooms and camping options, with hot showers. These can be booked through the club.

At the club, Marianne and I met three of our good friends, all of them outstanding paragliding and small-plane pilots (see photo opposite). They had completed an accelerated free-fall course there a few years ago. This course meant they never had to jump on static lines, which pull the chutes automatically and allow no free-fall time. Instead, they learnt to jump with two instructors each and got to free-fall and pull their own ripcords from the first jump.

If you are younger than 18, you will need written permission from your parents to skydive. Tandem skydiving has a maximum weight limit of 95 kilograms. All the instructors are certified with the Parachute Association of South Africa.

ANCIENT RUINS
The area also holds historical interest. The Lepalong Caves on Kleinfontein Farm, near Carletonville, were inhabited in the early 1800s by the Kwena people fleeing Mzilikazi. The Tolokwe Ruins are from an ancient Iron Age settlement; the Losberg hiking trail runs past them. The ruins of a Voortrekker fort are found on a hill known as Klein-Losberg.

ABE BAILEY NATURE RESERVE
Southern African Birding recommends the 4 200-hectare Abe Bailey Nature Reserve, near Carletonville, for spotting grassland and wetland birds. There have been 220 species recorded there, and its website states that you can expect to see at least 60 species in a morning.

IF YOU GO

When to go
Winter months, from about May to September, are best for skydiving in Carletonville, as the air is more stable. Summers can be wet and stormy.

Contacts and rates
• Skydive Joburg: tandem skydive ● (less if excluding DVD/photos); static-line course (one-day training, gear rental/first jump) ●; accelerated free fall (one jump with two instructors) ●. A non-refundable deposit ● is required at least a week prior to the jump. Tel 084 998 3178; web www.skydivejoburg.co.za; email info@skydivejoburg.co.za
• For details of the historical sites, visit the Merafong Municipality website, www.merafong.gov.za
• Abe Bailey Nature Reserve, www.sabirding.co.za

How to get there
Carletonville is less than an hour's drive from Joburg.

③ JOHANNESBURG: GREEN CITY

Mountain biking, zip lining, canoeing and stand-up paddling: the green parks and dams of Joburg offer enough outdoor activities to counter any level of big-city stress.

RIDING THE SPRUIT

Mountain biking gets addictive. You see athletes out early in the morning or after dark with headlamps in winter. Emmarentia is on one of the prime routes in Joburg: the Braamfontein Spruit, where there are about 40 kilometres of trails.

Across the city, 'weekend warriors' hit the river single track at dawn and unwind later at bike-friendly cafes. One Sunday I spotted five groups of Swampdogs riding along the Braamfontein Spruit. The Swampdogs are a relaxed biking club, one of many in Joburg, and I like to ride with them. As their late founder, Allan Laudin, told me: 'Mountain biking is not about the speed; it's about pleasure. This lifestyle has attracted a diverse collection of individuals, not clones in club kit but free-spirited lateral thinkers – men and women from 8 to 60, couples, singles and families.'

A typical Sunday ride starts on the Spruit at Fratelli's car park in Craighall Park. From there to Delta Park, across a bridge and up the hill through the trees, down the other side of Delta Park, across to Victory Park, towards Emmarentia, across the river, over tree roots, across to Albert's Farm towards Northcliff, then back towards Delta Park via a coffee stop at vida e caffè in Greenside, before heading back to Fratelli's. That route is about 20–30 kilometres, depending on which sections you include or leave out.

Joburg has many biking clubs and forums (for example, thehubsa. co.za), and Greater Johannesburg has several good mountain-biking routes, from Van Gaalen Cheese Farm, near Hartbeespoort Dam through to Northern Farm. Friends recommend places like Modderfontein Mountain Bike Park and technical bike parks to train at, like the PwC Cycle Park in Bryanston.

The 13 300-hectare Suikerbosrand Nature Reserve, south of Joburg, now has a mountain-bike route, to complement its hiking trails. Road

OPPOSITE: *Zade at Acrobranch*
ABOVE: *Claire paddling at Emmarentia and cycling in Delta Park*

cyclists train on the roads running through this reserve, and it must be one of the best on-road options in Joburg. I've done a route of about 70 kilometres on the road through the reserve a few times ahead of the 94.7-kilometre Momentum Cycle Challenge. (For more information about mountain biking, see page 175.)

GREEN CONCEPT, ON THE ROAD

Riding through Joburg on roads devoid of cars is what makes the '94.7' unique. But even more appealing to me is the Critical Mass ride, which takes place through downtown Jozi on the last Friday of the month.

If you're tired of your usual Friday-night routine, come hang out with the masses on bikes. Cyclists with fairy lights and neon strips, and jokers in masks and wigs are among several hundred riders who flood the streets. Motorists part like the Red Sea for the cyclists, and vuvuzelas blare in greeting as you pass through the inner city, then across the lit-up Nelson Mandela Bridge.

Critical Mass rides are a celebration of cycling in public spaces and raise awareness of the need for safe urban cycle paths. Cyclists in Johannesburg, Cape Town and Pretoria are finally riding this counter-culture wave, which started 20 years ago in San Francisco. Anyone can join, and strangers turn into friends along the way. There's a halfway stop for beer and pizza.

The ride starts in Braamfontein, where a party guy towing a boombox cranks up the beat. This ride is no

spinning session – you hardly raise your heart rate. Marianne and I did a longer variation, starting at the Dunkeld West Shopping Centre. We rode into Rosebank, past restaurants, through leafy Saxonwold streets, past the zoo and up to Constitution Hill. From Braamfontein, on the main route, we headed into Fordsburg and Newtown, where we had a social break at Mary Fitzgerald Square, waiting for the crowd to assemble as a single group. From Newtown, we followed a figure of eight: through the financial district to Arts on Main, then past Ellis Park and back through Joubert Park to Braamfontein.

Melvin Neale, one of the organisers, says only about 25 riders pitched for the first Critical Mass in 2007, but it was revived in May 2011 and is growing exponentially.

'Roughly 700 to 1 000 people turn up, and it spreads pretty much through word of mouth and social networking,' he says. 'Our marshals are volunteers and we are mindful nobody is left behind.'

The critical mass has been reached and I wonder how much bigger it can get. If you've got a bike – anything goes, from penny-farthings to recliners – come along to experience the city lights of Jozi with an adventurous cycling crowd.

STAND-UP PADDLING

Ku hoe he'e nalu, or stand-up paddling (SUP), has made its way from the giant waves of Hawaii to Johannesburg's suburban dams and lakes. SUP involves standing on a longboard and moving along by means of a paddle.

Cycling in Suikerbosrand Nature Reserve

Emmarentia Dam and its 100-hectare gardens are a gift to Joburg residents who wish to exercise in fresh air: you can paddle, swim, walk dogs, run, mountain-bike, play ultimate frisbee and picnic here. Amid the canoeists, canoe polo players and swimmers on the dam, you'll now also find SUP fans doing laps.

'For five years, I was the only one doing stand-up paddling here. Now many people are excited and trying it out,' says SUP instructor Gunter Berger, who runs equipment supplier Starboard SA. He also organises paddling at Germiston and Florida Lakes, and at the Homestead and Bronkhorstspruit dams.

On my first attempt at SUP, I

roughly midway between the nose and the back of the board. The paddle is like a spoon. If you're right-handed, you place your right hand at the top and your left below it. You dip the paddle into the water and pull, alternating sides. The movement is as simple as it sounds and it is easier than surfing, from which SUP originated. Gunter explains: 'Traditionally, surfing, which requires the right conditioning and technique, was male-dominated, but stand-up is much more accessible to women. It has hundreds of variations, such as flat-water paddling, wave riding and touring.'

This is why SUP is becoming increasingly popular, along with better views and staying dryer (in cold weather) than canoeists or surfers. SUP also works core abdominal muscles. And it's clear that it has become a lifestyle sport, like surfing.

WALK THE LINE: ACROBRANCH

Leaping out of trees or moving along monkey bridges in a lofty, leafy world gives you a new perspective.

The four courses set up in the trees at Acrobranch in the James and Ethel Gray Park in Birdhaven (within walking distance of Melrose Arch) – with cables and monkey bridges to balance on, nets to climb and zip lines to slide – are designed to appeal to children and adults.

The training course starts with cables close to the ground and each of the four courses ascends higher into the trees.

Before you start, you sign an indemnity form, then the guide gives you a climbing harness and three

expected to fall in, but beginner boards are surprisingly stable and it was possible to glide around on two different models without getting wet.

Like surfboards, SUP boards come in different shapes, materials, lengths and widths, and the greater your skill, the wider your options.

Gunter brought equipment for us to try out and showed us how to paddle. To balance, you place your feet about shoulder-width apart, devices – gear that will protect you if you fall. The two carabiners (metal clips) with reinforced material slings attached to your harness must be connected to the cables at all times. The third device is a pulley for sliding along the zip lines.

After kitting up, you step onto a low wooden platform and attach your carabiners to the steel cables. A blue tape shows you where to put them; a yellow tape shows you where to put the pulley. During the 10-minute training course, you learn how to attach the pulleys and slide safely to platforms. You then move on to the first course and subsequent levels with guides to monitor you.

Acrobranch encourages participants to take charge of their own safety and therefore build personal confidence, along with the balancing and motor skills required. My friends who rock-climb felt their kids were secure with the safety systems here, but other parents do not share this view. One parent commented on www.jozikids.co.za that safety was a problem, including the lack of helmets.

I hesitated when I saw how high my son would have to climb, albeit in a safety net, to do the longest zip line. But Zade, then five, wanted to do it and he ascended quickly to the 10-metre-high platform. (Zade, however, has already had exposure to heights.) Jumping off, he enjoyed the fast slide along the 250-metre cable, in tandem with a guide, and the next 140-metre slower slide to the ground. (Read more about zip lining as an activity and other places to do it, on page 198)

SHELLY HÜFNER

IF YOU GO

When to go
Critical Mass rides take place on the last Friday of every month, departing from Braamfontein. Canoeing and SUP are all-year-round sports, though the winter cold on the water can be daunting. Summer storms in Joburg force you to take cover as the thunder and lightning roll in. But you can be active all year round, and winter days can be sunny enough to strip down to a T-shirt.

Contacts and rates
- Acrobranch adventure park is in the James and Ethel Gray Park, Birdhaven. Open weekends, public holidays and school holidays 9 am–5 pm; weekdays 1 pm–5 pm, booking required. Each course takes two to three hours. Cost: adults ▪; children ▪, depending on child's age and size of the group. Tel 078 438 7463; web www. acrobranch.co.za; email bookings@acrobranch.co.za
- Critical Mass: for information, visit www.critical-mass.co.za; email melvinbike@gmail.com
- Dabulamanzi Canoe Club (Emmarentia Dam): Tel 011 486 0979; web www.dabulamanzi.co.za; email info@dabulamanzi.co.za
- Starboard SA: Tel 011 314 0795 or 072 612 6209; web www.star-board.co.za
- Swampdogs: web www.swampdogs.co.za; email swampdogsmtbclub@gmail.com

How to get there
All roads eventually lead to Joburg, whether you want them to or not!

WATERBERG: MOUNTAINS OF THE BUSH

4

LIMPOPO

Reddish mountains, plateaus and river gorges make the Waterberg, in Limpopo, stand out from most bush destinations, and it has the added attraction of being malaria-free. Game-viewing destinations are abundant in South Africa, but the Waterberg Biosphere exceeded our expectations in terms of wildlife encounters and natural beauty – and it feels untouched by habitation.

The various nature reserves and parks – from self-catering to five-star opulence – have hiking and mountain-bike trails through the bush, waterfalls and shimmering rock pools. The rock climbing here is an adventure if you're prepared to pioneer routes off the beaten track. Premier big-five reserves are close enough to towns like Pretoria and Polokwane for day visits. For the best game viewing, go in the sunny, dry winter season, but temperatures can fall to below freezing at night.

HANDS ON WITH AN ELEPHANT

An ecotourism experience with a bull elephant at Welgevonden Game Reserve in the Waterberg was a great opportunity for us. Game viewing tends to be wild, but not active, unless you're on foot or biking. Welgevonden is developing plans for 'voluntourism', and that's why Makweti Safari Lodge invited us to join them for a hands-on experience in Welgevonden.

This big-five reserve sustains two lion prides and we also saw elephant, rhino, many types of antelope and birds (there are 250 species in total) during our visit.

Scientists have been working for more than 15 years in the 37 500-hectare reserve, and now a voluntourism initiative – whereby guests contribute to and get involved with conservation – is on the cards.

We were allowed to join an exercise to remove a tracking collar from an elephant. Our tasks included helping to topple the darted bull, pouring

LEFT: *Chasing and darting an elephant in Welgevonden Game Reserve*

water over his ears to keep him cool and pulling off his collar, which was no longer needed two years after his vasectomy.

The ultrasound scan showed that the elephant's vasectomy appeared to have been successful. Job done, the vet gave the bull a jab to wake him up. He staggered to his feet and we watched him walk away, looking just as dazed as we were from our close-up contact with him.

RUNNING WITH RHINO, CLIMBING WITH PYTHONS

Rhino are among the attractions of another Waterberg destination, the Palala River Reserve, where we spent a night. When I went for a run the next morning in the reserve, I was on high alert for rhino, since they rule in this terrain.

Not far from here, at the Vista Vistas Private Nature Reserve, African rock pythons live up to their name. The reserve has warthogs and klipspringers, kudu, giraffe and leopard. My most impressive sighting, however, was the least expected.

Back in 2007, I went to Vista Vistas with a friend and expert rock climber, Mark Seuring, to explore the cliffs. We first hiked along the Mokamole River Gorge, which is good for swimming and fishing (yellowfish, black bass, kurper and catfish). In searing heat, we veered up through cacti to the rock face, and Mark started climbing. About 20 metres up, he found a python in a crack next to him. Stepping onto a knife-thin ledge to his left, he avoided the shelter where it was hibernating.

Usually cracks offer the easiest way

up a wall and when you climb at my level of ability, they are necessary. But this one was now off limits. Looking into the recess, I was startled by the size of this snake's coils. After we had climbed to the top, I was ready for a sundowner at our bush camp, Uitsig. As the stars came out, we could hear baboons barking, and what sounded like the faint roar of a lion drifted up to us.

BRAAI OR BOMA FEAST?

The Waterberg has an extraordinary range of accommodation, from affordable self-catering options in nature reserves and farms, to five-star, big-five lodges catering primarily to foreigners. But these lodges often offer last-minute specials or discounted rates to South Africans if you book within 48 hours of travel or if you book for longer stays.

Uitsig bush camp is the most secluded of the four options at Vista Vistas and has the best view. The two stone-and-thatch huts are at the top of a cliff. Each spacious hut, with practical decor, accommodates four people, and the bathrooms have hot water from a 'donkey' (a wood-fired geyser). A third hut houses the kitchen; the generator is set away from the accommodation. Uitsig is perfect for a group of friends wanting to escape to the bush.

If you want four-star food, visit the Entabeni Big 5 Reserve, about half an hour away. Entabeni has five restaurants and seven bomas.

Podica cottages, overlooking the Palala River in the Lapalala Game Reserve, are a great hideaway and the reserve has rhino. The round huts are open plan, each with a fireplace, and wood is provided. Outdoors we lit a fire and braaied for dinner, enjoying the peace of being on our own in the bush.

Nungubane Game Lodge, a thatch-and-stone lodge built on stilts, has great views from its deck, where you can enjoy fine food, and swim in the pool with views over the reserve. Each of the five charming chalets has its own deck and an outdoor shower. We thought Nungubane was good value for a big-five lodge and enjoyed

its stylish atmosphere. Nungubane's owner, Irishman Ian Finley, has published a book of wildlife photos called *Welgevonden*.

Watching a lion kill a warthog at the waterhole, metres from the lodge, was just one of the attractions to be experienced at Makweti Safari Lodge, which is unfenced. The proximity to big game, its location on the edge of a gorge and the limited number of guests (five suites) make it an exceptional destination. The suites are luxurious, built of stone and floor-to-ceiling glass. They have verandahs on stilts and some have plunge pools. Makweti is a member of the international gastronomic society the Chaîne des Rôtisseurs.

CYCLING WITH LIONS

The annual Mabalingwe Lion Man mountain bike race in the Waterberg in May attracts close to 1 500 riders – a tenfold increase since it started more than a decade ago. The Lion Man is the only race in a big-four nature reserve, although the riders of the tough 80-kilometre course are probably going too fast to do much game viewing. But along the sand and bush paths, I saw a giraffe loping (faster than me), elephant dung (what do you do if you see an elephant on a bicycle?), a warthog and birds. The lions, which I heard roaring in the night, were in another camp.

OPPOSITE FAR LEFT: *Claire helping perform an ultrasound and remove the sedated elephant's collar*
OPPOSITE LEFT: *Riding the slides at Bela-Bela, gateway to the Waterberg*

IF YOU GO

When to go
The Waterberg has three seasons. The wet season, from November to April, is hottest, but temperatures are not as high as in the Kruger National Park. May to July is dry and good for game viewing. August to October sees the temperatures rising. Malaria is not a problem in the Waterberg, one of the area's great draw cards.

Contacts and rates
• For details on the Waterberg, visit www.waterbergbiosphere.org; or to book, www.waterbergreservations.com
• Makweti Safari Lodge: last-minute rates (i.e. booked within 10 days of travel) are the best value; per person per night sharing ⚫. Tel 011 837 6776; web www.makweti.com; email makweti@global.co.za
• Mabalingwe Lion Man: Tel 014 736 9000; web www.mabalingwe.co.za; email info@mabalingwe.co.za/lionman@vea.co.za
• Nungubane Lodge: per person per night ⚫; specials available for longer stays and last-minute bookings. Tel 014 755 4928; web www.nungubane.co.za; email lodge@nungubane.com; for central reservations Tel 086 131 8887 or 083 707 7128; email reservations@nungubane.com
• Podica self-catering cottages, Lapalala Nature Reserve: per person per night on weekends ⚫; game drives per person ⚫. Tel 014 755 4415 or 082 570 8474; web www.jembisa.com/palala
• Uitsig Bush Camp sleeps 10; rates per night (weekends) ⚫. Tel 015 453 0693; web www.vistavistas.com; email vistas@mweb.co.za

How to get there
The Waterberg is two and a half hours by road from Johannesburg (Pretoria is about 45 minutes closer) and has two airstrips. Bela-Bela is the closest town to the N1 highway.

LIMPOPO

South Africa's northern-most mountain range, the Soutpansberg, often gets overlooked in favour of the more imposing Drakensberg. But like the reclusive cousin at a family gathering, the Soutpansberg has its own charms if you take the time to explore them.

Extending 130 kilometres from west to east, the Soutpansberg has sheltered people for centuries, with the San and Venda inhabitants leaving behind relics of their civilisations in its hills and caves. Besides the rock art, you can visit well-known archaeological sites, such as the former mountain kingdom of Thulamela, west of Pafuri, or discover hidden traces of the past.

We went walking in the Luonde Mountain Reserve, on the upper slopes of Luonde Mountain (formerly called Piesang Kop), and deep in the forest came across ruined dwellings, which were, according to Wits University researchers, the outposts of the ancient Zimbabwean empire. The six crumbling stone walls and enclosures are protected, and walks to this site require a guide.

A trail to a viewpoint near the top of Luonde is shown by coloured markings on rocks and trees. The Luonde Mountain Reserve belongs to several farmers. The owners of the Molozi farmstead, where we stayed as guests, have organised more than 50 surveys on the trees, shrubs, animals,

OPPOSITE AND ABOVE LEFT: *Claire and Marianne exploring the indigenous forests and trees in Molozi*

birds and snakes found in the reserve. The Vhembe Biosphere is registered by UNESCO.

Historical sites are only one of the attractions of this region. Tree and bird species abound, as we observed while hiking through the dappled Luonde Forest, which can become shrouded in mist. Soutpansberg Tourism says the sprawling range of hills has no less than 555 tree species – you can find 145 species at the Indigenous Tree Sanctuary in Makhado (Louis Trichardt) and about 540 types of birds. The number of birds is hardly surprising given the range of habitats here, from grasslands to different types of forest, acacia thornveld and riverine terrain. Among the birds we saw were the purple turaco, the scarlet-chested sunbird, the black-breasted snake eagle, the grey-headed bushshrike, the African paradise fly-catcher, the golden-tailed woodpecker and the black-headed oriole.

Walking along the Baobab Meander

One of the recommended birding sites is the 9 300-hectare Blouberg Nature Reserve (close to Casteel), which has a steep, 400-metre wall that ranks as one of the premier rock-climbing destinations in South Africa. The climbing routes at Blouberg are excellent, and when you climb in this remote region, you are more likely to spot Cape vultures than people.

The Blouberg Wilderness guided hiking trail opened in 2012 in the Blouberg Nature Reserve. KuneMoya manages this reserve, which has one of the biggest Cape vulture colonies and best vulture viewing points in the country. A so-called vulture restaurant (a feeding site for these endangered birds) affords visitors close-up observation.

The baobabs, tamboti woodland, fig forest and the Brak River floodplain are among the distinctive features KuneMoya lists in the reserve.

On our travels, we have been enchanted by baobabs, particularly in Botswana. These trees command your attention with their massive girth, witch-like branches and upside-down appearance, and we decided to follow the Baobab Meander route in Limpopo, near Musina. These giants are increasingly threatened, despite legislation protecting them. But as far as we know, no harm could come to a tree that size by climbing it. So I decided to scale a baobab with an especially wide trunk and use its bulges and hollows for footholds and handholds.

Once I stepped onto this tree, I found it to be more smooth and slippery than it looked. For every move up, I slid backwards. So for protection, a friend tossed a rope over a branch near the top of the tree and I put on my climbing harness (after swapping my skirt for Marianne's jeans) before trying again. The view from high up, as the sun was sinking behind us, was well worth the effort.

We had another memorable sunset when we went for a boat cruise past a lone hippo on the Albasini Dam. With a surface area of about 3.5 square kilometres, the dam is in a valley at the foot of the Soutpansberg, close to Makhado. The dam is popular for fishing; however, crocodiles compete for its carp and barbel, so swimming and contact water sports are out of bounds. On evening and morning boat rides, we saw these reptiles lurking near the banks. I wish I had spotted the 'white crocodile' of

Lake Fundudzi, a mythical creature, like the river python, described in VhaVenda stories. Lake Fundudzi, deep in the Soutpansberg Forest, is believed to be South Africa's only natural inland lake, but we have yet to make a trip to its shores and pay a ritual greeting to its gods.

SHILUVARI LAKESIDE LODGE AND SUNSET HOUSE

On the eastern shore of Albasini Dam is an alluring African-style lodge called Shiluvari Lakeside Lodge, which has a spa. We wandered around its peaceful grounds, admiring the sculptures by local artists, such as *The Resurrection* by John Baloyi, along its paths. Shiluvari features on the Ribolla Arts and Crafts Route, where works by the VhaVenda 'Big Five' artists can be found. It also has an artists' shed and offers guided tours to artists' homes.

The wraparound terrace overlooking the dam has an eco-friendly design and the swimming pool complements this. The thatched cottages are decorated in a rustic African style. Shiluvari's Wood-Owl country restaurant has won awards and its Hog and Hound pub has a fireplace for cold nights.

Shiluvari is proud to have been one of the first tourism destinations in South Africa to be awarded the Fair Trade in Tourism certificate.

Sunset House, on the opposite shore, is a self-catering thatched house with three bedrooms. The voluminous living room extends onto a deck with a view overlooking the dam and has a brick braai.

IF YOU GO

When to go
The Soutpansberg is wetter in summer than winter. Yet it tends to be a relatively dry region without extreme temperatures, making it suitable to visit all year round.

Contacts and rates
- Shiluvari Lakeside Lodge: rates from ● to ● per person sharing. Tel 015 556 3406; web www.shiluvari.com; email info@shiluvari.com
- Birders keen to rent Sunset House can contact the Molozi Agricultural Manager. Tel 015 583 0213; 015 516 4515 or 084 582 5585; email driesa@mweb.co.za
- Access to the Luonde Mountain Reserve can be arranged through the Molozi forestry manager. Tel 015 516 1489 or 082 901 2899
- Blouberg Nature Reserve: rates per adult ●, per child ●, per vehicle ●. Tel 078 869 5240; web www.kunemoya.co.za/blouberg.htm; email info@kunemoya.co.za
- To follow the scenic Baobab Meander, turn off the N1 towards Tshipise, north of Polokwane but before Musina (formerly Messina). You can visit the Baobab Tree Reserve at Musina.

How to get there
From Johannesburg, via the N1, it takes about three hours to get to Polokwane which is the gateway to Limpopo. The towns of Makhado and Musina are also on the N1 going north.

MAGOEBASKLOOF: MIST CONNECTIONS

6

LIMPOPO

Magoebaskloof, at the northern tip of the Drakensberg in Limpopo, has pristine rivers, lakes and mountains, and remains untrampled by tourists. To get an aerial perspective on this 'land of the silver mists', we went canopy gliding and explored the indigenous forest.

CANOPY GLIDING

Sliding along steel cables in George's Valley Gorge offers you a bird's-eye view of the dazzling waterfalls and rapids of the Groot Letaba River. If you paddled the river or hiked alongside it, you wouldn't be able to enjoy such exposure. Of the four canopy tours I've done – the others were in Tsitsikamma, Magaliesberg and Karkloof – I enjoyed Magoesbaskloof the most.

Before the canopy gliding (also known as zip lining) begins, the guides give a safety briefing. After signing an indemnity form, the guests are strapped into a harness and handed a helmet and gloves. Once kitted up, you walk down into the gorge and step onto the first platform. The guides attach you to the cables and then you're ready to slide down to the next platform aided by gravity; there is the option to brake if you like. We were lucky to be the only people on our tour and we floated along in a peaceful, meditative zone.

KIDS' PLAY

For young children particularly,

OPPOSITE AND ABOVE: *Canopy gliding in Magoebaskloof*

canopy gliding – the adult version of what we used to call 'fufi sliding' in my childhood – is a high-adrenalin adventure. The river runs far below and the cable above it stretches a long way from one platform to another – a distance of up to 140 metres. My son, who was five at the time, found it thrilling and wanted to go back for more as soon as we were back on the ground. He did three of the eleven slides alone, braving the leap-off and reaching the far side on his own. He also enjoyed the eight other slides in tandem with the guide, who made him feel safe and relaxed. The recommended minimum age is seven. (Discover more about zip lining and other places to do it on page 198.)

BACK ON THE FARM

We stayed at Kuhestan Farm, which borders indigenous forest on the Magoebaskloof Pass. From here we went cycling into the forest, following a hiking trail when we

could and carrying our bikes when it got too technical. We saw enormous indigenous trees – but could not find *the* big tree, despite following a sign; and I saw a bush pig as we cycled back to the farm.

Kuhestan has four comfortable cottages with flowering gardens overlooking the forest. Each cottage has a fireplace, wooden shutters and a patio with a braai.

Hosts Shahrzad and Brett Hone own the organic farm, which has an abundance of raspberries, avocados, fresh herbs and vegetables. They also produce cordials and preserves, and sell spices and traditional kilims. They offer Persian cuisine, and you can book ahead to eat there for a minimum of 10 guests. We spent an engaging afternoon in a cookery class, learning how to make six traditional dishes.

A MAGIC CULINARY CARPET

Unlike Marianne, I'm not into cooking. I'd rather compete in *Fear Factor* than *Master Chef* any day. But even I could not resist the invitation to do Persian cooking with Shahrzad. She left Iran when she was 15 but has created a Persian enclave at Kuhestan Farm with her husband, Brett.

Persian cooking is elaborate by any standard, so Shahrzad, Marianne and I started our 'cookout' mid-afternoon with a cup of freshly ground coffee to give us stamina.

The dishes took hours of pre paration. The main dish, *khoresht-e fesenjan*, a pecan and pomegranate casserole with chicken, looked like a brownish stew once cooked, but in the mix were delicacies such as crushed walnuts, pomegranate, molasses and saffron.

The other dishes were *nokhod polow* (rice with spices, herbs and peas), *challow* (saffron rice), *mast-o-khiar* (a cucumber side dish), *shirazi* salad (tomato, cucumber and spring onion) and *shir berenj* (rice pudding).

The food had distinctly exotic flavours and it wasn't hard to imagine this cuisine being served to the rulers of the Ancient Persian Empire.

FLOWERS AT SPRING FESTIVAL

The Magoebaskloof Spring Festival, from the end of September to early October, is famous for its array of flowers, particularly azaleas, crab apples and Japanese cherry trees.

The Cheerio Gardens and Sequoia Gardens have exhibitions and wine tasting on offer. The Magoebaskloof Hotel has an exhibition of rare orchids.

If you prefer beer, the Snyman Farm showcases microbrewery beers, and there are outdoor activities such as clay-pigeon shooting. Bavarian oompah bands and Welsh choir The Men in Red liven up the carnival, which revolves around Haenertsburg village.

Picasso's is a restaurant with a good range of options prepared by its Austrian chef.

IF YOU GO

When to go
Limpopo is warm, and hiking, kloofing and birding are good in at least three of the four seasons. In winter it can get cool.

Contacts and rates
- Canopy gliding: per person, including refreshments and lunch ⦿. Tel: 083 866 1546; web www.magoebaskloofcanopytour.co.za; email adventures@thabametsi.com
- Kuhestan Farm: per person per night sharing ⦿; one-day cooking course ⦿. Tel 082 903 7593; web www.kuhestan.co.za; email info@kuhestan.co.za
- For details about the Spring Festival, Tel 082 883 4449; web www.mountain-getaways.co.za; email haen@telkomsa.net

How to get there
Magoebaskloof is about three and a half hours' drive from Joburg (Pretoria is closer), near Haenertsburg, on the road east between Polokwane and Tzaneen.

KAAPSEHOOP: DREAM RIDES TO FREEDOM

MPUMALANGA

Hidden in the woods of Mpumalanga, where wild horses roam, lives a long-haired horse whisperer and a hermit with green fingers. Horseman and archer Christo Germishuys looks like an outlaw – a modern-day Robin Hood, at ease on any steed, with bow and arrow in hand. And he is equally skittish, disappearing as swiftly as the vagabond horses of Kaapsehoop when they run into strangers.

WILD HORSES

Kaapsehoop is known for its 200 or so feral horses, which roam the forest in bachelor groups and some larger herds. Christo runs Kaapsehoop Horse Trails, while his friend, Pierre van Zyl, who lives across the Berlin Forest, provides rooms and an outdoor kitchen on the edge of the escarpment for riders doing overnight trails. (For more information on horse riding, see page 188.)

Pierre survives mostly off the land at Coetzeestroom in the Blue Swallow Natural Heritage Site, where he grows vegetables and gathers firewood from fallen trees. These men exist outside the confines of society, and their days have a rhythm far removed from that of the digital world most of us inhabit. Marianne and I got a glimpse of this existence when we went to Kaapsehoop, which is half an hour from Nelspruit, to do a horse trail.

To get there, we took a gravel road through the forest, past stationary railway coaches, which form an overnight stop on the Kaapsehoop hiking trail, and past a forestry village.

OPPOSITE AND ABOVE: *One of the trails through forest and over the escarpment that leaves from the Kaapsehoop Horse Trails farm*

In a clearing we found the stables, paddock, four cottages and the Shirebeen pub/coffee bar. Little more than a wooden counter with a few stools under a tin roof next to the stables, the pub is surrounded by an astonishing collection of tree stumps, rocks and metalwork.

DREAMY TEAM

The Kaapsehoop trail manager, Mariska Redelinghuys, abandoned city life and school teaching to join the maverick team. Even Christo's horses are freer than most. They are not stabled at night and come in only for food, grooming and rides. The horses used on the trail rides are geldings or stallions, whose temperaments range from tame to free-spirited.

Marianne once had horse-riding lessons in Argentina with a gaucho, a pampas cowboy, so she was ready for a feisty horse. I had never had lessons and have been bucked off by several horses. So to be on the safe side for the first ride, Mariska gave me the tamest and slowest horse, a glossy giant called Baobab, and Marianne had a shire cross called Mazabuka.

Accompanying us were six dogs, including a brave mongrel terrier called Vlooi and a Malamute. We set out on an icy blue morning, walking slowly through the fields and passing the forestry settlement before winding up into the forest. We ambled through trees lit by shafts of green sunlight. Bird calls mingled with the sound of the wind. We stopped at the edge of the escarpment to enjoy the view and stillness. On more open sections we cantered, and the horses were sure-footed when descending steps in the forest. On the last leg back to the stables, we meandered through a Canadian maple forest.

Our second ride, the next day, was almost as peaceful as the first, but at a slightly quicker pace. We followed another route through the forest and the horse-and-dog packs moved along smoothly. Our horses whinnied when they saw wild horses and they let us move closer to have a look. Under their spell, we wound our way back to the stables.

Kaapsehoop is a dreamlike hideaway. I would imagine when the stables are shrouded in Kaapsehoop's legendary mist, you might drive away wondering if it really exists.

Kaapsehoop Horse Trails run five-day pony camps for children aged 8 to 15. The children go riding and hiking – exploring caves and waterfalls – and have fun working with the horses under supervision. The camps cater for a minimum of 6 children and a maximum of 12.

VICTORIAN COTTAGE

Lambourn is a self-catering Victorian cottage with a spiral staircase rising out of the open-plan living room and kitchen to an upper-floor bedroom with a skylight and a balcony. The three bedrooms have en suite bathrooms; there were fresh roses placed next to our beds and a complimentary bottle of wine.

The living area has a gas fireplace, which we needed in the misty cold when we arrived, and historic photos on the wall. The gardens in the front (with flowers) and back (aloes on the rocks) enhanced the charm.

STABLE COTTAGES

The Quinley Cottage, trail house,

stable house and guest house at the Kaapsehoop Horse Trails stables have wooden floors, old stoves and modern appliances. Black-and-white photos of horses adorn the walls while real horses wander around outside. The bird life is plentiful, and there are about 10 pairs of the threatened blue swallow.

The stables are on the Berlin forestry plantation, which borders on indigenous grassland.

DINE WITH GROOVY GHOSTS
The Bohemian Groove Cafe in Kaapsehoop is an outstanding restaurant/art gallery, with handmade furniture and paintings by Charl Fourie. He runs the place with his wife, Andrea, who is a talented chef. Famous ghosts swirl in the ether of this enchanting establishment. Reservations recommended.

BACK IN TIME
Establishments like the Silver Mist Country Inn and Koek 'n Pan pancake house offer substantial meals at a rural pace – don't be in a rush. The pancake house offers a range of large pancakes. Silver Mists, which used to be the post office and dates from 1898, is worth a visit. It is a beautifully restored and friendly establishment, but don't go expecting gourmet food.

GLASS GIFTS
De-liteful Glass Works, on the left as you enter Kaapsehoop, has a selection of rainbow-coloured glass products – from wind chimes to lamp shades and pendants. They also produce commissioned glass work, including windows and door panels.

IF YOU GO

When to go
Summer can be rather wet (which allows the forests to thrive) and winters are cool enough to light up a log fire.

Contacts and rates
- Kaapsehoop Horse Trails: per person per ride ⚫; rates for five-day pony camps per child (Monday morning to Friday lunchtime) ⚫.
  Tel 082 774 5826;
  web www.horsebacktrails.co.za;
  email info@horsebacktrails.co.za
- Stable accommodation: per person per night sharing ⚫; for guest house per night ⚫ (contacts same as above)
- Lambourn Cottage: per night for the cottage ⚫. Tel 073 675 8731;
  web www.kaapsehoop.com;
  email info@kaapsehoop.net
- Bohemian Groove Cafe:
  Tel 076 764 7625 or 013 734 4545;
  web www.bohemiangroovecafe.co.za

How to get there
The village is only half an hour from Nelspruit, which is served by Kruger Mpumalanga International Airport. It's about 290 kilometres from Johannesburg, turning off the N4 up a pass not far beyond Ngodwana.

WATERVAL BOVEN: REACH FOR THE DREAM

MPUMALANGA

Waterval Boven, on the edge of the escarpment in Mpumalanga, is an adventure playground with world-class rock climbing and mountain biking. Within 60 kilometres of this sleepy railway town, renamed Emgwenya and nicknamed Boven, you'll also find highly rated paragliding and fly fishing.

WHY GO?

If you've never climbed, abseiled or cycled trails and want to try, Boven is the ideal place to start. On reddish cliffs flanked by indigenous forest overlooking the Elands River Valley, with waterfalls along the river, there are over 700 climbing routes – from staircase easy (grade 9) to insanely difficult (grade 34). (Find out more about rock climbing and the different grades on page 178.) Adventure company Roc 'n Rope, based in Boven, has an outstanding track record of safely introducing hundreds of people to climbing, abseiling and mountain biking over the past 13 years.

But Waterval Boven is more than just an outdoor-activity destination. The place has a magnetism that wins the hearts of climbers and mountain bikers who come to explore it. Many relationships have begun under its starry skies and weddings have been celebrated at its sandstone crags. Another favourite activity nearby is trout fishing in Dullstroom (40 kilometres away). And FlyBambi,

OPPOSITE: *A friend, June Fabian, climbing at Waterval Boven*
ABOVE: *Rock faces and mountain biking*

about 20 kilometres away off the N4, is one of the country's premier paragliding launch spots. In summer, when it rains, the rapids in the Elands River rise and experienced kayakers take to this creeky river. (Read more about kayaking on page 171.)

If you come to Boven, you're sure to find activities that keep you, and any children, happy.

PERSONAL EXPERIENCE

I discovered Boven a week after I had moved to Joburg from the coast. Missing the surf, I drove out there to try to find someone, anyone, to take me climbing for the first time. About three hours later, I met some students, who invited me to join them. My first-ever climb was exhilarating, and from the moment I stepped onto the rock, in a borrowed harness and barefooted, I was addicted.

Nearly 20 years later, I still spend weekends here, and Marianne and

I, and our partners and friends, have spent many a New Year in Boven together. One New Year's Eve, after feasting with Gustav Janse van Rensburg and his French wife, Alex, who have become good friends over the years – they run Roc 'n Rope – we decided to go night climbing.

Even with head torches, it was difficult and we started that year on a natural high long before the champagne was flowing. More typically, many climbers at Boven start their day with a mountain-bike ride.

ACCOMMODATION
Self-catering
The Climbers' Lodge in the town appeals to backpackers, and it can be booked for groups.

This stone 'chateau' has three rooms with six bunk beds (duvets and pillows supplied) and four small rooms with double beds below the outside deck, which is built of railway sleepers.

The three showers have river pebbles on the floor. The kitchen is well equipped (wine glasses, for instance). The lounge has beanbags, a ceiling fan and a fireplace.

Another self-catering option is Fruwink, which consists of sandstone railway cottages in town, which have curious interleading rooms and communal kitchens.

Tegwaan, a country getaway on the outskirts of Boven, has two stylish cottages and a garden.

There is more traditional accommodation in town, like the Shamrock Arms, which also has a bar and a restaurant.

Camping, safari tents and chalets
The aptly named Tranquilitas is an attractive and safe camping destination above an arc of cliffs, with views over the valley. Tranquilitas has camping, safari tents and self-catering chalets. The campsites have a few power points and fire pits, and the ablution blocks have hot showers.

OPPOSITE AND ABOVE: *Climbing and mountain biking in Waterval Boven*

The six safari tents have two beds, crockery and cutlery, a power point and tables.

This adventure farm also has four comfortable chalets, each with a double bedroom, a large cupboard, two single beds and a table in the open-plan kitchen. The chalets are small but a covered outdoor patio with another table and chairs, and a stone-built braai, make up for this.

The wide lawn and trees, jungle gym, swings and swimming pool, with an artificial climbing wall at one end, mean that children can run wild at Tranquilitas.

But it is also a great place for low-action (maybe a spot of tightrope walking) or zero-action weekends: stretch out in a hammock in the sun or just relax in front of your chalets.

IF YOU GO

When to go
May to September are great months to climb and bike in Mpumalanga, although the nights can get cold in Boven, as it is on the escarpment. In May, Boven is still green after the summer rainfall and not too hot.

Contacts and rates
- For accommodation (Tranquilitas, The Climbers' Lodge, Fruwink and Tegwaan) and climbing trips and courses, contact Roc 'n Rope Adventures. Tel 013 257 0363 or 082 753 3695; web www.rocrope.com; email climb@rocrope.com
- Tranquilitas: camping per person per night ◉; safari tents per night ◉; chalets per night ◉; web www.tranquilitas.com
- The Climbers' Lodge: dorms per person per night self-catering ◉; per night for a double room ◉
- Tegwaan: per person per night ◉ for a minimum of six people sharing
- Fruwink: per person per night ◉. Tel 012 331 3062 or 072 147 3862; email bezroos@iafrica.com

How to get there
Waterval Boven is just off the N4 highway, 90 kilometres from Nelspruit and roughly 260 kilometres from both Pretoria and Johannesburg. The official name of Waterval Boven is Emgwenya but road signs still refer to Waterval Boven.

WHITE RIVER: GATEWAY TO KRUGER

⑨

MPUMALANGA

White River, in the Crocodile River Valley, Mpumalanga, is a flowery town that offers the best of both worlds: outdoor and bush activities are as accessible as its restaurants and spas. Only half an hour (30 kilometres) from Kruger National Park's Numbi Gate, White River has mountain biking in the forests around it and paddling on its doorstep.

OPPOSITE AND ABOVE: *Mountain biking at Mankele*

Established in the early 1900s after the Anglo-Boer War, White River, whose name reportedly derives from the milky colour of a local river, has evolved from a marginal settlement to a thriving town, a hub for fruit, nut and timber plantations – and tourists – according to the website Mpumalanga Happenings. Kruger Mpumalanga International Airport is nearby and Nelspruit is about 20 kilometres away.

IN HARMONY

The rolling landscape around Nelspruit and White River is being developed rapidly and the Mbombela Stadium, built for the 2010 FIFA World Cup, is one of its landmarks. The stadium was designed to be in harmony with the bush and its orange roof supports are shaped like giraffes. This distinctive arena is worth a visit during a major sports or music event. I attended an Africa Cup of Nations match there in 2013.

In contrast to the noise of the match, I stayed in a peaceful bush estate along with the resident blesbok and purple louries.

I ate out in one of the town's fancy 'lifestyle centres'. On the lawn next to one of these centres, a small group clambered out of a helicopter one morning. Apparently, chopper owners fly in to White River for breakfast. And I saw another helicopter on the banks of Lake Longmere, where I went canoeing with friends who live on the bush estate. They are among a wave of newer residents who have migrated east from Joburg in search of a more outdoor and balanced lifestyle.

WILD RIDES

Despite the large number of townhouse developments on the outskirts of town, it is still easy to escape into nature. For example, I did a mountain-bike ride with my friends, and the trail traversed rivers, a washed-away bridge, a rocky uphill path through macadamia-nut orchards and gum plantations, and mud and more mud. Our ride was marked by bundu bashing and we sustained bloody scratches. From a sloping rocky dome at Emily's Beacon, we had an exceptional view into Kruger, and we aim to ride along the fence in wintertime.

In summer, White River swelters and Lake Longmere, north of town, is a haven where you can canoe for miles upriver from the Lowveld Canoe Club on the lake.

Come the summer rains, Mpumalanga's rivers begin to run and the white-water paddling on the

Crocodile, Sabie and Elands rivers takes off. My friends have been canoeing and kayaking along the creeky, rushing Elands River. I went rock climbing on short, bolted routes on a dome at Bundu Rock Resort, where you climb above the forest and have panoramic views.

MANKELE

Mankele Mountain Biking, near White River, is an activity park with amazing colour-coded bike trails – from novice to highly technical. If you're into riding, go visit with friends or family. (For more information about mountain biking, see page 174.)

The park is surrounded by indigenous forest and the Crocodile River runs next to it. It has an open grassed area, as well as an obstacle course with high wooden boardwalks. There are camping areas laid out across the grass and in the bush on the periphery. Log cabins with decks and braai areas are set among clearings at the edge of the forest.

ABOVE: *Fish spa at Sudwala Caves near Mankele*
OPPOSITE: *Chilling at the log cabins after a ride at Mankele*

Short circular trails, like the smooth five-kilometre single-track route, which is great for children, follow the park's perimeter. This winds through bamboo and trees, past a stream – where I saw a mother and baby duiker at dawn – over muddy crossings and back into the 2.4-kilometre 'adventure zone'. This track was fun to ride, with sloping half circles, berms and jumps, and helped improve my confidence.

The 20-kilometre blue route, which we did one afternoon, was an outstanding ride. This trail was well designed and maintained, with a variety of riding challenges and warning signs – but nothing too technical. Alongside the trails are chicken-run detours.

We cycled through forest, over bridges, through tunnels, up a long climb, through plantation forest, into the open with landscape views, and down into a flowing track through a forest tunnel, which had bends and steady drops, requiring concentration. We rode back into the park at sunset. We'll definitely be going back.

MALLARD COTTAGE

A fish eagle in flight above the dam at Waterberry Country Estate and placid zebra are among the wildlife you are likely to see driving to Mallard Cottage on Coral Tree Way. Fever trees and untamed bush make Waterberry feel more like a game park than a residential estate, and the houses are set well apart.

A self-catering cottage overlooking the dam, Mallard has two attractive en suite double bedrooms facing onto the lawn. Waterbirds and other types abound in the vivid garden. Between the bedrooms is an open-plan kitchen and lounge, which opens onto a covered patio with a braai.

This is tranquil accommodation and many guests come back after their first visit.

Dilly's Suite is a guest wing on the owner's house, with a private entrance and patio, and a comfortable double room.

GANACHE CAFE, ZANNAS AND SHAUTANY CHOCOLATIERS

Exotic names, fine food and plants – these White River establishments are worth a visit:

Ganache Cafe, in the courtyard of Casterbridge Lifestyle Centre, serves cappuccinos with gingerbread men. Casterbridge is a collection of shops, restaurants, an art gallery, museum, theatre and a boutique hotel. The works of local artists and potters are displayed in designer shops whose prices seem to cater to foreign tourists. But Ganache is value for money: our cooked breakfasts were beautifully presented and tasted as good as they looked.

Shautany Chocolatiers, next door, has home-made Belgian chocolates.

The Bagdad Centre, across the road from Casterbridge, is another place with specialised shops and fresh, organic food. Zannas Flavour Junction is a deli with a bakery and gourmet salads.

White River has several nurseries. The White River Garden Pavilion is a relaxed place for adults to eat with kids, who can also play on the jungle gym next to the tables.

IF YOU GO

When to go
Spring, summer and autumn are glorious months in this part of the Lowveld. Mid-summer can get hot, but not unmanageably so.

Contacts and rates
- For more information, visit www.lowveldtourism.com or www.mpumalangahappenings.co.za
- Lowveld Canoe Club: Tel 083 452 7549; web www.lowveldcanoe.co.za; email secretary@lowveldcanoe.co.za
- Mallard Cottage: per unit (four people) ● ; Dilly's Suite sleeps two (per unit ●). Tel 013 751 1024; web www.mallardcottage.co.za; email cottage@mallardcottage.co.za. On long weekends, and school and Christmas holidays, the rates go up.
- Mankele: log cabins sleep up to eight; per adult ● ; per child ● ; minimum per night ● ; permanent tents per adult ● ; minimum per night ● ; camping per adult ● . Tel 078 801 0453; web www.mankele.co.za; email ride@mankele.co.za

How to get there
White River is 20 minutes by road north-east of Nelspruit. Mankele is 30 minutes west of Nelspruit by road, six kilometres off the N4 on the R539.

10

KRUGER NATIONAL PARK: WALKING WITH RHINOS

MPUMALANGA/LIMPOPO

Standing still won't usually make your heart race. But when two young white rhino bulls walk towards you in the bush, you shift onto high alert.

When we were on a rhino walking safari in the Kruger National Park, a grazing pair of rhino approached our group, as if they were coming to inspect where we ranked in the pecking order. Below them, that's for sure. When they got too close, ranger Mark McGill signalled that we should scramble onto a nearby termite mound with thorn trees. We hastily joined Marianne on the top of the mound, and the noise we made startled the bulls into running away. Once they had reached a safe distance, we watched the pair resume their meal unperturbed.

Watching endangered rhinos in their environment was a privilege. These magnificent herbivores, particularly the black rhino, could become extinct unless poaching is stopped. Healthy adult rhinos have no natural predators. Only man. In 2012, 668 rhinos were killed by poachers in South Africa – almost two a day – and the killing continues unabated (in 2013, the toll was 367 by the end of May). For more about walking safaris, see page 193.

OPPOSITE: *Ranger Mark McGill dishes the dirt on creatures great and small*
ABOVE RIGHT: *Plains Camp*

SOLE SAFARI

We saw rhinos every day during our three-day stay in the Mutlumuvi private concession in the Kruger National Park, where Rhino Walking Safaris operates. We saw five on our first morning drive, along with 10 sables.

Our most memorable sighting during a game drive was a newborn rhino calf. Only a day or two old, it looked like an overgrown puppy flopping along under its mother's belly.

Mutlumuvi shares an unfenced boundary with the private game reserves of Mala Mala and Sabi Sand, and is only 20 minutes from the Skukuza rest camp. What is special about this 12 000-hectare wilderness area is that there is almost no vehicle traffic, which is great when you're tracking the big five on foot.

TRACKING

At dawn, after coffee, tea and rusks, we set out walking. Mark pointed out

rhino, leopard and lion spoor, though we never saw any of the big five on foot on our first day. We did, however, see a wild peach tree, bent and worn smooth by a rhino rubbing its rear against it.

We also walked past several rhino middens, dung piles they leave along popular routes to send messages to each other. Males mark their range by scattering their dung and spraying urine into the bushes.

In line with Kruger regulations, we had to hike away from one of the 'little five' – a lone baby buffalo, which tried to follow us. We hoped its mother would find it before the predators did.

Mark showed us how to weave a rope from the bark of an acacia tree and warned us about the poisonous bark of the tamboti tree. On each of the three hikes we did over two days, we learnt about the insects, birds, mammals and trees in that terrain. We learnt about the behaviour of the smallest creatures, such as termites and communal spiders, and the giant land snail, as well as elephants and rhinos. We also saw the smallest carnivores in the park, a pack of dwarf mongooses scooting out of their termite den.

We also spotted a range of raptors – the African hawk eagle, a tawny eagle, a brown snake eagle, white-backed vultures, scops owl and Verreaux's eagle owl.

SLEEPING IN THE TREES

This concession has three camps, taking a maximum of 16 guests, and we spent a night in each. The Rhino Post Safari Lodge has a deck and bar overlooking the bed of the Mutlumuvi

River, and luxurious rooms. Plains Camp has exquisite views, a colonial-style outdoor lounge and permanent safari tents with fine finishes.

But the wild Sleepout Camp was our favourite. We got to our 'sleepout' shortly before dark on the second day, just in time to see our tents, which are perched high in the leadwood and marula trees. This unique camp, operated by Rhino Walking Safaris, is built on wooden platforms in the canopies of trees.

Above intermittent thunder, we could hear lions roar and watched two males swagger down to a watering point near the camp. The lightning illuminated them and, after drinking, they stretched out, apparently unperturbed by the storm.

As we braaied, we heard a hyena cry from the camp while the lions kept roaring. Mark told us how he had heard lions and hyenas fight over a kill right under the platform on which we were sitting.

FOOTLOOSE

As a child, Mark came to Kruger for his family holidays and joined its staff in 2001. 'I have been here ever since. From 2006 to 2008, I worked in anti-poaching. For eight months, I followed six white rhinos after their release,' says Mark, who intends to use his pilot's licence to combat poaching. But for now he's happy to move through the bush on foot.

And the freedom of being on foot, inside the Kruger National Park, tracking the big five and discovering its lesser-known creatures, is what sets Rhino Walking Safaris apart.

IF YOU GO

When to go

The best time for game viewing in Kruger is during winter when the animals search out the waterholes and rivers. The bush is greener in summer and the rivers bigger, but it gets extremely hot (well over 30 °C) and wildlife is harder to spot.

Contacts and rates

Rhino Walking Safaris is run by Isibindi Africa lodge. Rates per person sharing per day, including accommodation, meals, walks and game drives, wines, beers and soft drinks, from ⬤. Tel 011 467 4704 or 467 1886; web www.isibindiafrica.co.za/rhino-post/index.htm; email info@rws.co.za

How to get there

You can fly to Kruger Mpumalanga International Airport (in Nelspruit) from Durban, Cape Town and Joburg. From Nelspruit to the nearest Kruger gate, Numbi, is about an hour's drive. From Johannesburg by road it takes four to five hours to Numbi Gate.

11

KOSI BAY: WILD WONDERLAND

KWAZULU-NATAL

The swamp forests of Kosi Bay are bewitching. You almost expect the trees to start moving and whispering, and water nymphs to rise out of the shimmering lakes, of which there are four linked by a network of river channels.

The area was originally named the Greater St Lucia Wetland Park; it is now known as the iSimangaliso Wetland Park. The dark waters of this hidden world are unlike any place we'd seen before our trip there. We felt as if we'd stumbled onto location for a *Survivor* series, except that the remote inlet, from where we were launching our canoe, was deserted. The sole reminder that these wetlands are inhabited was a rudimentary ferry, made with branches of raffia palms tied together with vine ropes, with a long rope attached.

Thonga fishermen, who lived in the park long before it was declared South Africa's first World Heritage Site, still inhabit the swamp forest and catch fish using traditional bamboo traps first used 700 years ago. When we were on the lake, we saw a fisherman poling along in a handmade dugout canoe.

We had arranged to explore the lake system by canoe and were expecting a long paddle. We were surprised, therefore, at the start of our exploration when our guide, Vusi Mahlangu, pulled out only one paddle.

OPPOSITE AND ABOVE: *Paddling on the lake systems near Kosi Forest Lodge*

Clients are usually guided, so he was astonished that we wanted to join in, but he agreed we could take it in turns to paddle, which worked out to our advantage when the wind got up.

To reach the lakes, we hiked through pristine forest with Zulu potberry trees, forest-climbing bamboo, iron plums and creepers, and enough open space to appreciate the environment. In this sandy forest, you can walk easily without getting entangled or having to duck at every bend. We learnt about the milkberry tree, whose fruit, when it ferments, intoxicates monkeys so that they fall out of the trees.

After hiking for about 20 minutes, we reached the water's edge and a bulky Indian canoe was retrieved. Its size made the paddling demanding but also meant the canoe was stable when waves rocked it. We pushed off from the shore and headed up the Siyala River. From this perspective, we could admire the swamp forest

CLAIRE KEETON

VUSI MAHLANGU

TOP AND ABOVE: *Marianne relaxing at Kosi Forest Lodge and both of us aboard a traditional ferry*

with its giant raffia palms, ferns and sprawling swamp fig trees that hang over the banks. We drifted through purple water lilies – Vusi made us necklaces by entwining them together – passed a kingfisher and saw a leguaan and a palm-nut vulture in the trees.

When we had gone upriver for some distance, we headed back towards the lake system. I took over the helm and paddled us towards lake four, which is freshwater. Lake three consists of 20 per cent salt and 80 per cent sweet water. By the time we reached lake three, the wind was whipping up white horses on the surface so we stayed close to shore, as we headed towards lake two. But the narrow channel between lakes three and two is long, and we turned around before we reached it.

We heard a splash in the water while we were cruising along and looked around to see a young hippo – not a croc, as expected. Soon after this, we were back at the bay where we had set off and our trip was over. Long afterwards, however, we maintained our sense of wonder at these unique wetlands.

KOSI FOREST LODGE

All eight canvas, wood and thatch suites are designed with privacy in mind. Sitting on the deck (which has a hammock), overlooking a secluded glade, you hear birds and monkeys, and the occasional thunderstorm. The rooms are charming and rustic. They are also comfortable – with fine linen, carpets and mosquito nets, though the space is limited and they have no electricity. At night, paraffin lamps are lit in the rooms and there are bamboo torches outside.

My favourite feature was the outdoor bathroom built around an imposing buffalo thorn tree. Showering or bathing under the sun or stars is fabulous. The suites have an inside toilet and basin (useful when it's pouring with rain).

The meals at the lodge are enticing and excellent, and the kitchen caters to the special dietary needs of guests. The dining area is on a deck in a forest clearing and there is another deck with a lounge.

Across from reception is a deck in the trees with a fireplace. A short distance away is a swimming pool overlooking Lake Shengeza. At night, hippos graze around that side of the camp.

IF YOU GO

When to go
Summers on the KZN coast get humid as well as balmy, but if you're in the forest or on the water at Kosi Bay you'll be cooler, and on the ocean you may catch a sea breeze. Winters are very temperate with low 20s during the day – and the mercury is unlikely to dip below 12 °C.

Contacts and rates
Kosi Forest Lodge: rates per person per night sharing (January–March) ◉; April–August ◉. Includes all meals, tea and coffee, canoeing, a guided walk in raffia forest and a sundown experience. Tel 035 474 1473 or 035 474 1490; web www.isibindi.co.za/kfl; email res@isibindi.co.za

How to get there
You can fly into the mining and yachting harbour of Richards Bay and drive two to three hours north-east to Manguzi (the small town closest to Kosi Bay). It is about a four-hour trip from Durban up the N2, and about seven hours from Joburg on the N17 and N2 highways.

12

DURBAN: BEACHFRONT LIFE

On the Durban beachfront at sunset you will find adults and children on the promenade trying out every type of sport, from rollerblading to boxing, in a scene that conjures up Hollywood images of LA's Venice Beach. The Moses Mabhida Stadium is a distinctive landmark in this beachfront sports precinct, as is the uShaka Marine World water park.

KING SWING

The Moses Mabhida Stadium is impressive, particularly when you're standing on a narrow ledge near the top, getting ready to jump across the pitch far below.

My decision to do the big swing was impulsive. When I realised we could ascend in the sky car, climb the steps of the soaring arch to do the jump and be allowed to walk across the pitch at the end, it just seemed like a good idea.

Big Rush Urban Adrenaline, which started operating in February 2010, claim theirs is the only stadium swing, and the highest swing in the world. 'Jump into the void 106 metres above the World Cup football pitch and swing out in a huge 220-metre arc under the iconic arch', is their siren cry. It's all true: the void, the adrenalin and the sensational swing.

After I'd signed up, my guide locked me into a full-body harness. Then we walked towards the sky car, which takes up to 20 passengers. The sky car rose on the sea-facing side of the arch to a viewing platform.

We exited the wide platform onto the steps of the arch. (On the south side, you can do a 550-step adventure walk along the 350-metre arch, secured by a cable.) We walked towards a platform below us.

From the steps, I climbed down a ladder onto a metal platform. Luckily for me, the Big Rush team were well organised and I didn't have to wait to jump. I know from experience the easiest way to bungee or king swing is not to think twice about it.

So after looking out over the pitch and feeling a surge of adrenalin, I leapt out. It was both exhilarating and peaceful once I was flying through the air. Too soon, the guides hauled me up to the platform and we descended the remaining steps to the ground.

To exit, we were allowed to walk across the pitch of the stadium, named after a former leader of the South African Communist Party.

ON THE MOVE

When Marianne and I went to try rollerblading on the Durban promenade, we saw the usual walkers, runners and cyclists, as well as swimmers and surfers. Swelling their numbers was an aerobics class, people doing boxing training on the grass, skateboarders showing off their tricks in a skateboarding park and, looking the most slick of all, rollerbladers.

Our rollerblading efforts were less successful, though we did avoid collisions with the speed-skaters. Marianne has some experience and she managed to glide along looking competent. I had spent no time on rollerblades and, having depleted my adrenalin for the day, was unwilling to take a hard fall, so I edged along slowly. Once we'd had enough, we had cocktails at the beach cafe Circus Circus.

USHAKA MARINE WORLD

uShaka Marine World, further along the beachfront, is a kids' paradise. This marine park has the biggest aquarium and the steepest water slide in the southern hemisphere, and shark diving and ocean walking.

uShaka has three fast water slides,

with the highest being the 18-metre Drop Zone (tip: hold your nose closed on the descent or it'll be filled with water), and they were fun.

Marianne and I took a double tube and twisted down the whitewater of Dizzy Duzi into the river channel that flows through the park. We floated along for 450 metres, past penguins and fish tanks.

Then it was time for an ocean walk. This gives people with no scuba diving or snorkelling experience the opportunity to go about three metres below the surface. You wear a bell-like helmet, which rests on your shoulders, into which air is piped from the surface through tubes. Before you start, you get a safety briefing, sign indemnity forms, and then you are fitted with a rash vest with padded shoulders and booties to protect your feet.

Once we got to the tank, we had the helmet placed onto our shoulders and descended one by one down a ladder into the water. During the descent, we had to keep unblocking our ears like you do when you're diving. On the bottom, we stayed to one side of the tank, as instructed. We saw stingrays and numerous other fish, including barracudas.

SHARK DIVE

After the ocean walk, I went to the shark enclosure to do a shark dive. You climb into a cage and get dragged on a pulley to the middle of a tank, in which ragged-tooth, white-tip reef, dusky and sand sharks are circling. The sharks and brindle bass soon distracted me from the cold I was feeling.

The top of the cage is above the surface, so it's easy to breathe and you stay under for as long as you can hold your breath. You are warned not to put your fingers through the cage, which is fitted with rails you can use to help you submerge yourself.

It felt peaceful lying there watching the sharks, none of which seemed interested in me. However, this was nothing like the experience of cage diving in the ocean at Mossel Bay or Gansbaai (see pages 104 and 164), where great whites lunge towards you. But it is a good opportunity to observe sharks in their element.

uShaka has a large aquarium – designed around a shipwreck modelled on a real wreck off Durban – with many exhibits and tanks. As well as the displays, ocean walk and shark diving, you can interact with dolphins and watch a dolphin show or watch the penguins and rays being fed.

GIBA GORGE

If you're ready to leave the ocean, Giba Gorge, on the outskirts of Durban, is a family-friendly mountain-bike park.

Giba has more than 30 kilometres of outstanding trails, and those we followed, including combinations of the Switchback Alley, Shayamoya and Waterfall routes, were well cut. They wind among trees and along slopes and sharp turns.

For hard-core mountain-bikers, Giba has black routes and big-air permanent dirt jumps, which look wild. The easier jumps are designed for children but the biggest are for professionals only. Giba also has a BMX track.

The trail centre and KTC Bike Shop rent out and sell bikes, and any other biking gear you might have wanted for Christmas but didn't get. You pay the park entrance fee at the centre and rent bikes at the shop, whose staff also do repairs. Use of a bike wash bay and hot showers are included in the day pass.

Family members and friends can enjoy the picnic spots or hike around the gardens and up to the waterfall. Giba also has a coffee shop with fresh food, an art gallery and an indigenous nursery.

SHARK'S VIEW

My favourite place to stay in the city is a self-catering establishment on the hill in Morningside. Shark's View has two options – the Studio and the Loft, both with air conditioning and free Wi-Fi.

The Studio is spacious, with a bedroom and a roof fan. It has a kitchen and living area with satellite TV. The en suite bathroom has a shower. The Studio opens onto a pool patio with a braai.

The Loft is more like a writer's eyrie with a distant view of the ocean. It has a slanting roof and a bed with a skylight above. The bath in the en suite bathroom has a view, and there's a shower. There is a kitchen, and the lounge has satellite TV.

Shark's View is owned by Mike and Ruth Behr, who are climbers. Mike was involved in the construction of uShaka and has won a Mountaineering Development and Training Trust award for guiding.

IF YOU GO

When to go
Gautengers and other landlocked holidaymakers flock to Durban in winter, when the weather is cooler but sunny. In summer Durban gets steamy.

Contacts and rates
- Durban Tourism: Tel 031 582 8242; web www.durban-tourism.com
- Big Rush King Swing: per person ◼; Tel 031 312 9435; web www.bigrush.co.za; email bookings@bigrush.co.za; Sky Car tickets per adult ◼; children under 12 ◼; children under six free; the cars run 9 am–5.30 pm; Adventure Walk tickets ◼; children must be over 10 (the Adventure Walk is available only Saturdays and Sundays)
- uShaka Marine World offers the following tickets: Sea World for the aquarium; Wet 'n Wild for the waterworld (both of these are ◼, for adults and for children aged 3–12); or Combo for both (adults ◼, children ◼; the shark cage experience per person ◼; the Ocean Walk is ◼ per person; more details at www.ushakamarineworld.co.za
- Giba Gorge Mountain Bike Park: rider's day pass for adults and children under 12 ◼; family members' non-rider's pass ◼; Tel 031 769 1527; web www.gibagorge.co.za; email info@gibagorge.co.za
- Shark's View: per person per night ◼. Tel 082 388 0100; web www.sharksview.co.za; email ruth@sharksview.co.za

How to get there
Durban has a large new airport (King Shaka International), half an hour north of the city, with flights to and from most major centres in the country. The city is six or so hours' drive from Joburg on the brilliant but busy N3 highway.

13 HOWICK & KARKLOOF WATERFALLS

KWAZULU-NATAL

In the rolling fields of the KwaZulu-Natal Midlands, Marianne and I went chasing waterfalls and we found two shimmering cascades in forests, not far from each other. In the green hues of summer, the Midlands have elements of the English countryside on a greater scale, but indigenous and plantation forests break up its cultivated appearance.

We mountain-biked to the Karkloof Falls, following brilliant trails to reach it, and rock-climbed on the steep cliffs next to the Howick Falls in its spray. We've both been climbing and cycling near Howick for years and it's always exciting. But this was our first time riding the graded single-track routes in Karkloof, although I had cycled before in the Karkloof Classic mountain-bike race.

The starting point for this event and the trails is the same: the Karkloof Country and Polo Club. During the May mountain-bike festival, the club gets overrun with mountain-bikers getting ready for the various races: 60, 40, 20 and 10 kilometres (for kids). The Classic also has night and enduro rides.

On the 40-kilometre race, we had been diverted up into the forest over logs because of swarming bees on the planned route. That's the difference between mountain-biking and road races: you never know where you'll end up. But on the weekend of our trip, we weren't sure where to begin. Horse riders – not bike riders – were

OPPOSITE: *Marianne climbing next to the Howick Falls*
ABOVE LEFT: *Crossing the river above the falls*
ABOVE RIGHT: *Claire cycling in the Karkloof forests* PICS: JAMES PITMAN

the only people we could see at the club. As we set out with our friend, James Pitman, a pair of mountain-bikers arrived and showed us that the trails started across the dirt road from the paddocks and clubhouse.

The Karkloof mountain-bike routes were perfect for us – among the best we've ever ridden. They are fast and flowing, with wide loops on the Boomslang Trail, and hairpin turns, and places you can jump if you know how to on the Soulfly section. Rocky and narrow sections, obstacles and bridges ensure your attention doesn't wander on the routes, many of which wind through Sappi forests.

Most routes have been graded according to difficulty – green, blue and black diamond (the hardest) in line with International Mountain Bicycling Association standards. The

TOP: *Claire abseiling down the Howick Falls*
ABOVE: *Marianne cycling towards the Karkloof Falls* PICS: JAMES PITMAN

Karkloof guide states that 'the revered Gauntlet (black diamond) is a large eroded valley made traversable by bridges and high switchbacks'. We're intermediate riders who don't have technical downhill skills, so we were on green and blue trails most of the time. However, hard-core routes are mapped out.

Our route connected with the River Riviera Trail, which winds along a grassy path by the Karkloof River. From here, we detoured down to the falls and played around in pools on slick rock at the top. From this spot, we rode back to the club. The quality of these routes is enough reason for any keen mountain-biker to pay a weekend visit. (Read more about mountain biking on page 174.)

As a bonus, we also went climbing at the Howick Falls, which are much higher and steeper than those at Karkloof. We found that the magic of climbing routes while a hundred metres of water roars next to you had not diminished with time.

James, who builds small planes and flies them around the world, has a family farm in Howick, and we first climbed there several years ago. At Howick Falls you start by abseiling down to the ledge from where you begin. If you find climbing up impossible, you could abseil further down to the pool, swim across it and walk the Gorge Trail. This hike, which starts to the left of the viewing platform looking out to the falls, drops down to the pool.

But the most thrilling route is up, with the falls pounding down next to you.

STAY WITH STUDS ...

Shafton Grange Guest House and Lipizzaner Stud is a peaceful 52-hectare farm with a stream. The farmhouse, with five en suite bedrooms, has a verandah and vast lawns.

You can hear the horses from the rooms and a pair of crowned cranes have nested in a dead oak tree. We booked the guest house when we did the Karkloof Classic and spent a festive weekend there. Craig Rogers, who runs Shafton Grange with his wife, Kelly, cooked us a fine roast for Sunday lunch.

... AND WHISTLE WITH WEASELS

Notties pub, with its wooden panelling and fireplace, is a popular institution in the Nottingham Road Hotel. Patrons flock to its big-screen TV during sports events. The food is standard pub fare, but the hotel restaurant has an à la carte menu.

The Nottingham Road Brewery, next to Rawdons Hotel, has an impressive range of ales, including Tiddly Toad Lager, Pickled Pig Porter and Whistling Weasel Pale Ale.

IF YOU GO

When to go
In summer the Howick and Karkloof waterfalls are most impressive but conditions for outdoor sports may be wet. Autumn and winter are cooler and drier.

Contacts and rates
- Shafton Grange Guest House: rates per person per night sharing, self-catering ▣; per person per night sharing B & B ▣ (extra for dinner, if requested). Tel 082 749 9117 or 082 872 0883; web www.shaftongrange.co.za; email info@shaftongrange.co.za
- Howick Falls: to climb or abseil with a guide at Howick Falls, contact Peak High. Rates per day ▣. For route information, contact the KwaZulu-Natal section of the Mountain Club of South Africa. For details, contact Gavin Raubenheimer on 082 990 5876; web http://kzn.mcsa.org.za/climbing or www.peakhigh.co.za; email gavin@peakhigh.co.za or mcsakzn@gmail.com
- Mountain-bike trails: Karkloof has a useful mountain-biking website, www.karkloofmtb.co.za. To ride (or walk and run) the trails, you must sign an indemnity form at the country club and pay a fee per day. For more information, email the Karkloof Mountain Bike Club at karkloofmtb01@gmail.com

How to get there
Pretty country roads, with more than a few bends, wind into the KwaZulu-Natal Midlands, passing the microbreweries and crafts outlets of Nottingham Hill. Howick is just off the N3 highway, two hours from Durban, and four to five hours from Joburg. The Karkloof Country Club is less than half an hour outside of Howick.

14

TUGELA RIVER: ZINGELA SAFARI AND RIVER COMPANY

KWAZULU-NATAL

The Zingela bush camp, on the banks of the Tugela River, is wild, despite the mowed grass and rustic bar overlooking the rapids. Zingela's owners, Mark and Linda Calverley, live in this idyllic environment encircled by acacia thornveld and cliffs – and maybe that's why Zingela has soul. The couple established the Zingela Safari and River Company 30 years ago, raised three children here and still run the operation.

When we visited recently, Felix the meerkat was the star of the camp, eclipsing even the mighty Tugela River. Eight-year-old Felix had been saved from a fire and has a damaged paw. His sister Lily was eaten by a python at the age of three – possibly the same python that river guide Danie van Zyl pulled out from under his baby's cot and the one his three-year-old son, Lee, grabbed by the tail.

SOUL SAFARI

We didn't find any snakes but we did see buck, including kudu, bush buck and impala, near the camp. The bird life is also impressive: besides fish eagles, we noticed the trumpeter hornbill, bald ibis, yellow-billed kites and bee-eaters.

Interestingly, Mark also has a sounder of European wild boars. We went on a late-night 'pigging expedition' with him, to toss slop to dozens of piglets and juveniles. The adult boars are bush-wise enough to stay away from safari vehicles.

The operation has a hunting concession, which is used to cull the

OPPOSITE AND ABOVE: *Paddling down the Tugela in the rainy season*

excess game and help keep the place running. Zingela's guides also offer abseiling, fly fishing and mountain-biking trips.

But the essence of Zingela is the river: this camp is the perfect base for kayaking or rafting trips, and the Tugela is one of South Africa's best and most consistent whitewater destinations. (To find out more about whitewater rafting and kayaking, see page 158.)

HOW BIG IS THE RIVER?

That's what we wanted to know as we crossed the bridge near Colenso in KwaZulu-Natal. The Tugela rises quickly after heavy rain, and is a powerful and scary river when it is high. When we'd booked around New Year, the water was overflowing onto the lawn of the camp.

We had already experienced the potential danger on two previous trips with friends. Those had involved rescues, a mutinying crew and a swimming spitting cobra, whose venom temporarily blinded a friend. We had also been hammered by rapids on a stretch of the Tugela during a whitewater-rafting championship. This time Marianne and I and friends were hoping for a mostly chilled time with some adrenalin. That's exactly what we got: enough big waves and churning whitewater to have fun without being intimidated.

TRIPPING THE TUGELA

On our first day, we rafted a stretch of river from the camp down to an easy take-out on Warthog Island, without flipping or falling out. The next day we asked if we could borrow kayaks and start higher up the river. Of our group, I was the least experienced in a kayak, which requires greater skill than a raft, having paddled one only once on a trip 10 years ago in Nepal. Marianne had better control, though she nearly

Kayaking the Tugela PIC: PIERS PIROW

drowned in a kayak a few years ago.

Our three guides, Danie van Zyl, Vince Venter and Jackalus Mbongiseni Mkhize, took us to a bend further upriver, just before a rapid called Marula Bend. At the start we were advised to paddle to the side of a rock to avoid the foam pouring over the rapid. I went straight over the rock, into the hole and out of my kayak, bumping on rocks. Despite the swimming I had to do on this stretch, I loved the trip past the cliffs, Finger Rock, the Ledges, the Pumphouse, and ending on Warthog Island. The island belongs to Zingela and has clearings under trees. There is a wood-fired boiler for those who camp out there.

LARNEY LANE, THE BADLANDS AND LIVING HIGH ON THE 'HOG'

Zingela's main camp has rooms of canvas, river stone and reeds, which create a rustic effect. We stayed in Larney Lane, behind the dining area. Larney Lane has comfortable, spacious

rooms and beds with mosquito nets. The rooms lead onto large outside showers. The furniture comes all the way from Zanzibar.

Marianne was out in the Badlands. These chalets are higher up the hill, with a view of the river, and more open to the bush (so expect insects). They are attractive, and also have nets and outdoor showers.

J-Camp, with its own bush kitchen and dining area, is popular for groups. Zingela also has an old farmhouse and a honeymoon suite. In all, Zingela can take up to 61 guests.

We really enjoyed the peaceful atmosphere and sundowners on the river. When we come back, we want to book Warthog Island and stay there with friends. We will still have to come upriver for a meal or two, though. The bush kitchen run by Linda was leagues above the usual river fare, with home-baked muffins and bread, gourmet salads, venison dishes and a full carvery among the highlights on the menu.

IF YOU GO

When to go
For big rapids and exciting river rafting, go in summer after the rains. That's the best season on the Tugela: high water and warm weather. It gets hot, so light bush clothing is advised.

Contacts and rates
- Zingela: average price per person per night, fully catered ◉
- Warthog Island (to book the whole island per night) ◉
- Rafting per person for a full day ◉
- Tel 036 354 7005/7250; web www.zingelasafaris.co.za; email zingela@futurenet.co.za. Phone and cellphone reception is limited, so try the satellite phone on 087 802 0050.

How to get there
To reach Zingela, you drive about four and a half hours from Joburg, or two hours from Durban, to the nearest town of Weenen. The final 26 kilometres to Zingela, on dirt road through thorny bushveld, takes about an hour and Zingela offers transfers to guests.

15

THE DRAKENSBERG: UP THE MAGIC DRAGON

KWAZULU-NATAL

The Drakensberg, or uKhahlamba (meaning Barrier of Spears – no doubt the jagged peaks like the Devil's Tooth gave rise to this Zulu name), soars to over 3 000 metres above sea level on the escarpment. The tallest peak in South Africa's highest mountain range, known as Thabana Ntlenyana, is 3 482 metres.

Ezemvelo KZN Wildlife manages the uKhahlamba/Drakensberg Park, which curves from north to south like a reverse sickle in the central Drakensberg. The 260 000-hectare park is a World Heritage Site that forms the border between South Africa and Lesotho. It is recognised for its natural and biological diversity, and rock art. Gazing at rock-art treasures like Eland Cave (only accessible with an accredited guide) in the Cathedral Peak Wilderness Area, it's easy to see its wonder.

A WALK IN THE CLOUDS

The fastest way to the top of the escarpment I know is a contour path that starts below Sentinel Peak, in the Mont-Aux-Sources region of the northern Drakensberg. The path zigzags steeply at first and then levels out to a gentle gradient, but it has a few narrow, exposed drop-offs. I hiked up it with my son, Zade, then five, in ominous weather and clouds. I stopped with him not far below the two chain ladders that lead to the summit.

From the top of the escarpment, the Tugela River drops into the 950-metre-high Tugela Falls, the second highest in the world. Zade had walked smoothly until then but it started to drizzle and we had only a few hours of daylight left. So I climbed the rest alone while my son went down with my friend, who, being an adventure racer and triathlete, had already run to the top.

To complete the round trip at walking pace, you need about five to six hours, starting from the Witsieshoek car park. At the ranger's hut you must complete the mountain register for your own safety and check the weather in advance. Ezemvelo limits the number of visitors to the summit to 50 overnight hikers and 50 day visitors.

CAVES AND KLOOFING

The Cathedral Peak area has 12 caves where hikers can stay overnight; Didima Gorge has enjoyable kloofing. As a journalist in the mid-90s, I was invited to join a wilderness therapy trail organised for traumatised

ex-child soldiers from the Thokoza and Katlehong townships. Watching the transformation of these teenagers as they hiked and swam through Didima Gorge, and the healing they experienced in the Drakensberg, was a remarkable experience. Didima Resort has a San Rock Art Centre, which provides information on the history and culture of the San people, whose art adorns many caves in this area.

RIDE, COWBOY, RIDE

When you pack a book, toothbrush and change of socks in a saddlebag on your horse for an overnight trip to Lesotho, you feel like you're leaving civilisation behind and heading into the Wild West.

The trail from the Bushman's Nek border post near Underberg (how often do you get to cross a border post on horseback?) into the Sehlabathebe National Park is roughly west into largely unpopulated territory. It is

also a steep ascent and the superbly trained Basotho ponies from Khotso Horse Trails were the best steeds we could have wished for on the rocky paths. These sure-footed beasts climbed roughly a thousand metres with us on their backs, and on the plains at the top they would run and gallop at the first chance.

This was by far the most exciting horse ride we have experienced. After about four hours on horseback – with a scenic stop for lunch – we reached a lodge with a fireplace at the top, which used to be visited by the prime minister of Lesotho. From here we wandered around the escarpment under the Devil's Knuckles and found an extraordinary boulder garden and wide tarns.

Back at the lodge, we had freshly baked Basotho bread and curry (an improvised bunny chow) for dinner, and in the morning were served coffee and oats. On our second day, we rode the horses to the Tsoelikane

Falls before reluctantly heading home. We were following an old donkey trail and this was a truly wild trip. If you have time, there are longer trails and you can see rock art and stay in villages.

CHAMPAGNE CASTLE

The Champagne Valley of the central Berg is also a popular horse-riding destination, with several stables offering guided trails. Marianne and I rode with uShaka Horse Trails run by Monk's Cowl Adventure, a centre that also has mountain bike trails. The horses were placid, and we walked, trotted and cantered through fields and forest.

I have ridden speedier horses from the Champagne Sports Resort up tracks with spectacular views.

KHOTSO ADVENTURE FARM, IKHAYA LODGE, MISTY PEAKS

Khotso has a relaxed backpackers in a farmhouse with bunkrooms, two self-catering rondavels and a big log cabin on offer. 'Don't let so much reality in your life that there's no room left for dreaming', is written near the fireplace in their lounge with an honesty bar.

Ikhaya Lodge, on a working farm with stables, is a self-catering farmhouse with large rooms and two rondavels.

For a private and luxurious self-catering getaway, visit Misty Peaks, which is in an eco-estate next to the Drakensberg Sun Hotel. Stone Villa, a three-bedroom house, has a spacious outdoor living area, braai and deck overlooking indigenous forest.

IF YOU GO

When to go

The Drakensberg is a destination for all seasons. In spring the flowers run riot; by summer the streams are flowing and the mountain pools fill up. Winter is snow season: if you pick your weekend, you can build a snowman or tackle ice climbing at Giant's Castle. But when the wind blows on the escarpment, it gets freezing, so go prepared with proper cold-weather gear.

Contacts and rates

- For bookings and information, phone the Ezemvelo KZN Wildlife reservations office, Tel 033 845 1000; web www.kznwildlife.com; email bookings@kznwildlife.com; for Injasuthi, Tel 036 431 9000; for Cathedral Peak, Tel 036 488 8000
- Mont-Aux-Sources: day visitors pay a permit fee ▪ (adults and children)
- Cathedral Peak/Didima Gorge: camping for two adults ▪; Monk's Cowl: camping for two ▪; Injasuthi: four-bed cabins per night ▪; Thendele: four-bed cabins per night ▪. For tariffs, check www.kznwildlife.com/index.php/bookings/tariff.html
- Khotso backpackers dorms ▪ per adult; doubles ▪ per room; camping ▪ per adult; horse trails overnight ▪. Tel 033 701 1502; web www.khotsotrails.co.za
- Misty Peaks: per night, accommodating seven adults ▪. Tel 036 468 1158 or 083 580 2682; web www.mistypeaks.co.za or www.accommodationdrakensberg.co.za
- uShaka Horse Trails: per hour ▪; tel 036 468 1136; web www.monkscowl.com

How to get there

By road the central Berg is about five hours from Joburg and about three from Durban. Try to drive during the day to avoid livestock and potholes.

16

HARRISMITH: SOUTH AFRICA'S MOUNT EVEREST

In 1924, when British mountaineer George Mallory was asked why he wanted to climb Mount Everest, he famously replied: 'Because it is there ... what we get from this adventure is sheer joy.' Nearly a century later, adventurers still feel this exhilaration. And South Africa's own Mount Everest, near Harrismith in the Free State, has its own magnetism. Of course, the local Everest is of a different magnitude to the world's highest peak. But after climbing in the region of both Everests, I think our own also has enduring appeal.

BAIE MOOI RAVE CAVE

When you enter Mount Everest Game Reserve, three ochre mountains rise out of the plains ahead of you.

Two have the sugarloaf and tabletop shapes distinctive of the Free State. The third peak resembles the profile of an eagle's head.

For a few years, when Americans owned the 1 000-hectare reserve, this was known as Eagle Mountain Game Farm and was off limits to casual visitors. In 2012 this climbers' destination opened up again, with boundless potential for active travellers of any age, including caves, trails, rock climbing, horse riding and biking, as my son, Zade, and other children have discovered.

The evening we arrived, Zade, then six, went climbing on a boulder next to our wooden chalet. At dawn the next day, he was out game watching and spotted springbok, zebra and wildebeest. Along the trail, he and Lindi Mthiyane, who was keeping an eye on him, unearthed jawbones, leg bones and other bleached remains.

Meanwhile, Marianne and I drove across to the main vertical face of Mooihoek Mountain. Roughly 150 metres up is a huge cave, nicknamed the Rave Cave, where we have camped many times. We decided to climb a new, easy route to the cave rather than the more technical, classic line we know well (Fight the Feeling, grade 21).

If you like heights and exposure, you could be guided up Rhino on the City Hall Steps (grade 14) even if you have no climbing experience. The moves are easy – imagine walking up very steep, tiny stairs with handholds to keep your balance – and the rock is solid, not always the case with Free State sandstone. Unlike many approachable routes, this rock is mostly clean, and not overgrown with lichen, moss or plants.

At the top we scrambled over to the cave, from where we abseiled down to solid ground. (Read more about rock climbing and what you will need on page 179.)

In warm weather you can swim in the dam, which has a fufi slide, or in the swimming hole.

NEED ALTERNATIVES?

That afternoon we went hiking to the lee side of Mount Everest, out of the wind, to an area known as Alternative Crag. In the past, we used to look down on rhino from here – but no longer. However, the reserve does have 22 species of game, including blesbok, waterbuck, bush pigs and anteaters.

Before sunset we went down for a horse ride. Zade and Lindi jumped onto two sedate horses: these farm horses are not going to win any derby but they are a safe introduction to riding.

We saw the dens of a colony of giant girdled lizard, known as the sungazer or *ouvolk* of the Free State, although we didn't spot them.

EAGLE MOUNTAIN

Mountain biking along paths and gravel roads is fun, and we cycled towards the Eagle Mountain at

---

OPPOSITE: *Claire preparing to abseil from the Rave Cave*

Claire climbing at the Mount Everest Game Reserve

sunrise on our third day. Single-track trails are likely to be cut but when we went, the biking was mostly dirt roads through the bush.

After breakfast we followed one of the footpaths from our chalet towards the Eagle head. This neglected trail was once a well-marked hiking path with wooden steps on steeper sections, and it is easy to follow. We ended up at a climbing crag known as Pocket City. Here you need to hook your fingers into holes (known as pockets), some big enough for only one finger, as we found out. After 15 years of camping and climbing in the reserve, this was our first time on this wall.

Everest has such an abundance of paths, rock faces and even a hidden kloof at the back of Eagle Mountain that you can keep going back to discover compelling new features.

ARTY GREEN DORPIE: VERKYKERSKOP

An alchemy of imagination and hard work have transformed the grimy outpost of Verkykerskop, about 30 kilometres down the road from Mount Everest (and about 45 kilometres north of Harrismith) into a refuge that gleams like gold under the Free State sun.

In the middle of nowhere, Verkykerskop, which has attracted musicians like Chris Chameleon, was evolving into a 'green living', artistic colony when we visited in 2007. Festivals, flea markets and exhibitions have marked its metamorphosis from a pit stop to a weekend destination. The people behind this regeneration were Matt Hoffman and Beth Hillary, who used only old and recycled materials in restoring this historic trading post to its present glory.

But don't drive too fast in the fading light along the R722, or you will miss this *dorpie* in the 700-hectare conservation area of Aansluit Landgoed – it is no more than a few buildings scattered along the road.

SMILEY'S AND REKORD JAZZ BAR

The landmarks of the village are the General Dealer, old post office turned art gallery, the Umgidi Backpackers, the Rekord Jazz Bar turned hotel and the Afsluit Guest House, where we stayed. An upgraded police station and ugly petrol station are signs that Verkykerskop inhabits the 21st century, even though its atmosphere conjures up bygone eras.

Smiley's Restaurant & Bar, a room off the General Dealer, is decorated in much the same style as the store. A retro mix of wood-and-glass cabinets, an antique chewing-gum dispenser, metal signs, solid old furniture, porcelain figurines and a cow's hide on the floor all contribute to the shabby-chic decor. The breakfast was excellent and Sunday roasts are a draw card.

Alongside the General Dealer is a restored mealie mill and next to it a wood workshop, which has been converted into a space for theatre and weddings. Within this workshop there are artists' studios overlooking the mountains. Not too far along the R722 is the Witkoppen Fish and Game Reserve, where musicians and artists hang out.

ACCOMMODATION

Mount Everest has comfortable Swiss-style chalets hidden away on mountain slopes and next to imposing boulders. The well-spaced-out campsite provides some seclusion. The chalets and campsite have braai areas.

In Verkykerskop, Afsluit Guest House is an Edwardian stone mansion with a broad porch running around it. The beautiful interior, with four bedrooms, has wooden floors and antique furniture. Off the kitchen is a boma with a central fireplace.

IF YOU GO

When to go
If you're going climbing in Harrismith then spring and autumn are good. The winters get cold, particularly if the wind blows, and the summers are hot.

Contacts and rates
- For information concerning Mount Everest, Tel 079 886 3101; web www.goeverest.co.za; email info@goeverest.co.za
- Rates for the chalets: per night for a four-sleeper chalet ▪; for a 10-sleeper chalet ▪; camping per person per night ▪
- Day visitors welcome: adults and children ▪
- A guidebook to rock-climbing routes is available at Everest reception but you need your own equipment and need to book a guide independently
- For a climbing guide, contact Gavin Raubenheimer: Tel 082 990 5876; web http://kzn.mcsa.org.za/climbing or www.peakhigh.co.za; email gavin@peakhigh.co.za or mcsakzn@gmail.com
- Afsluit Guest House: per person per night ▪ with a minimum charge for the weekend ▪; Tel 073 282 4840 or 076 458 3344; email: admin@verkykerskop-adventurezone.co.za
- Umgidi Backpackers: per person per night ▪
- Outpost Inn: per person per night ▪
- Verkykerskop Tourism, Tel 058 625 0071 or 079 873 0470; web www.verkykerskop.com; email matt@zippnorth.co.za

How to get there
Harrismith is in the Free State, and is a major stop midway between Durban and Johannesburg on the N3 highway.

FREE STATE

The Free State village of Clarens is known for its art galleries, brewery and coffee – but the Ash River nearby, which flows like gold-green champagne, and mountain trails for biking and hiking, are equally compelling reasons to visit. In mid-winter Clarens is a comfortable base for day trips to AfriSki in Lesotho, and cherry-picking excursions to Ficksburg, only a pip's throw away, are organised during the cherry festival in November.

About 20 kilometres from the Golden Gate Highlands National Park and encircled by the Rooiberge mountains, Clarens offers cultural, culinary and adventure activities in astonishing proximity. The 'jewel of the eastern Free State' is also only about three to four hours by road from Johannesburg, Durban and Bloemfontein.

OUR EXPERIENCE

The Ash River, which has a few big rapids (grades 3 and 4), and plenty of easy ones, as well as meandering stretches on which children can raft with no risk of flipping, was Clarens's major attraction for us.

Unlike many South African rivers, rafting on the Ash takes place in all seasons, as its level doesn't depend on rainfall. The crystal water comes from the Katse Dam in Lesotho's Maluti Mountains, through the Trans-Caledon Tunnel. I rafted this river about a dozen times when I was training on it with the South African women's whitewater rafting team in 2005, and with friends, including Marianne, one New Year's Day – and it's always fun and always cold.

Clarens Xtreme, an adventure company run by a charismatic ex-cop turned Rasta called Oliver Esplin, offers rafting down the Ash, and they guided us. Oliver has long dreadlocks and mixes Afrikaans, English and Sesotho in his enthusiasm to share the wonders of his mountainous backyard.

If you want a caffeine shot to prime your body before your adrenalin river rush, visit Highland Coffee, a few doors down from Clarens Xtreme. The coffee is roasted on site in the Millery Bakery and the out-of-the-oven croissants go well with the cappuccinos.

RAFTING THE ASH

On a deck at Clarens Xtreme, Oliver introduced us to our two guides; then we drove about half an hour to the river with them. The pair qualified on the mighty Zambezi River and instilled confidence with their professionalism.

After a safety briefing, we put in our boats just below a massive weir and practised our strokes with the spray floating over our heads. We set off in fast-flowing and sometimes narrow channels. Following clean lines through the rapids, we moved swiftly down the river.

The Ash River has 17 rapids on this section and we ran about half of them on our half-day trip. The steepest, tightest drop was on Bridge Rapid, a foaming channel that requires precise steering. If not, you swim.

After successfully running this rapid, we clambered onto the rocks for cooldrinks and cherries. Below Bridge Rapid, the river ran gently, so my son, Zade, and a friend joined us in the raft. Our peaceful drift along past willow trees, high banks and kingfishers was interrupted occasionally by horseflies.

Oliver wants to involve as many people as possible in the adventure sports he loves – the oldest rafting client Clarens Xtreme has had was 86 and the youngest was 6. The trip was over too soon and Marianne and I wished we had planned a full day. (For more information about whitewater rafting, see page 168.)

BIKING AND HIKING
But we had other activities lined up, including mountain biking with Oliver.

The first route we did was about 10 kilometres on the mountainside behind the town, with views over the valley. From a forest track, we climbed up the contour until we reached slick rock. After riding across the sometimes slippery rock, we cruised back onto a gravel road and did a

final climb into the town.

The second ride started from a cave in the mountains, where we had slept overnight. We traversed hills, ridges and rocky roads. The route was rough in places but not technical, and had sweeping vistas. We rode for about 45 kilometres and were hot and hungry by the time we got back to the Millery Bakery, where we wolfed down Danishes with coffee, followed by English breakfasts.

While we ate, another group was preparing for a cross-country motorbike trip, and tourists were checking out the zip line while kids played on the jungle gym. Clarens is also a popular fly-fishing and horse-riding destination.

CHERRY PICKING IN FICKSBURG
During the annual November cherry festival, wine-red and rosy-yellow bunches adorning Ficksburg's orchards are mostly ripe and easy to pick from the ground.

Ficksburg is the cherry capital of South Africa, and orchards of Napoleon, Emperor Francis, Rainier and Giant Hedelfinger cherry trees abound on farms around the town and its nearest neighbour, Fouriesburg. And when you've had enough hard labour picking them, take a cruise on the *White Mischief* with friends along the Meulspruit River through a private game reserve. This barge does breakfast runs, lunch outings and sunset excursions.

The river snakes below golden and red sandstone cliffs, dropping down to bush and wetlands in which wildlife proliferates.

EAT, EAT SOME MORE, DRINK AND BE MERRY

Restaurants abound in Clarens, giving tourists options from pizza to gourmet food. For heartier fare, the Highlander pub and restaurant is popular. The pizza, steak, lamb and duck dishes we had were substantial and, judging by the number of patrons, widely appreciated.

The Lazy Gecko serves light pancakes with a range of savoury and sweet fillings. Valley Cats had outstanding desserts, like a nutty fudge cake and exceptional lemon meringue pie.

CLARENS BREWERY

Clarens Brewery is a rustic pub/micro brewery on the town square and a vital stop if you're a beer drinker, and there's a microbrewery festival in February. A cherry cider made from Free State crops is one of three ciders the local brewery produces and makes available for tasting, along with its five ales. The cherry, mixed berry and apple cider were more sweet than dry. The English Golden Ale and Clarens Red were the favourite beers among our group. The brewery also produces stout and weiss beer.

ACCOMMODATION: MILLPOND HOUSE

Millpond House is an oasis – far enough from the crowds in the centre of town for guests to feel the peace of the countryside, but close enough to walk to the main square. It has large, classically furnished rooms and a garden overflowing with roses in summer. The hosts were friendly and their breakfasts memorable.

IF YOU GO

When to go
Clarens is popular at any time of year; spring and autumn are pleasant, while winter can be cold. If you're going rafting on the icy Ash River, summer is most enjoyable. If you want to pick cherries in Ficksburg, aim for November.

Contacts and rates
- For details on accommodation and outings in Clarens, www.infoclarens.com or www.clarenssa.co.za
- Clarens Xtreme: whitewater rafting per person for half day, including drinks ▣, full day including lunch and drinks ▣; mountain-biking trails ▣ (cost varies according to trail). Tel 082 563 6242 or 058 256 1260; web www.clarensxtreme.co.za
- Millpond House: per person sharing including breakfast ▣. Tel 058 256 1530 or 082 851 0131; email merri@millpondhouse.co.za
- For details about the Ficksburg cherry festival (from November), contact the tourist office, Tel 051 933 6486; web www.cherryfestival.co.za
- To book a trip on the *White Mischief*, Tel 082 920 5551; email gavin@thewhitemischief.co.za. Cruises per person plus entrance fee to the private reserve ▣.

How to get there
The roads to these Free State towns are generally good. Clarens is off the N5, roughly halfway between Joburg and Durban – a convenient place for friends from both cities to meet up.

GARIEP DAM & SMITHFIELD: CATCHING THE DRIFT

18

FREE STATE

Gariep Dam on the Orange River, voted South Africa's tourist town of the year in 2010, is 200 kilometres south of Bloemfontein, making it a popular halfway stop just off the N1 route between Joburg and Cape Town. This holiday village and yacht basin, on the western shore of South Africa's biggest dam, has more to offer than water sports, fishing and sailing. The Gariep Dam airfield is famous for gliding: world records, including distance and speed, have been set here and it has flown the flags of many nations.

CLAIRE KEETON

Just over 100 kilometres from Gariep is another 'halfway to anywhere' stop, which is how the frontier town of Smithfield presents itself. Smithfield is an idyllic overnight stop on the N6, halfway between Johannesburg and East London. It is also close to Bloemfontein, and worth a visit even if you're going nowhere.

SOARING WITH A FISH EAGLE: GARIEP GLIDING

Soaring in a two-seater glider with a fish eagle flying nearby is a rare privilege I experienced at Gariep Dam.

Glider pilots, whose graceful aircraft do not rely on engines, can share the space with eagles, in awe of their acrobatics. And from a distance, gliders glinting against a blue sky are just as mesmerising. When Marianne and I saw a 'flock' of these metal birds as we drove along the R701 from Smithfield, we took an unplanned turn off the road to the local airfield. The airfield's operations manager is Keith Ashman, an expert glider pilot, who enthusiastically offered to take me for a flip.

METAL BIRDS

Gliding is an unusual fusion of a solitary activity and teamwork. Glider pilots usually fly alone but they need a team to get airborne.

With their long, tapering wings, gliders are designed to gain altitude and stay in the air, as long as conditions and the pilot's skills permit. For every metre a glider descends, it can glide for 60 metres, compared to a conventional small plane where the glide ratio is around 1:4. This makes gliders one of the safest craft to fly and, when flying with an experienced pilot (Keith had 7 300 hours of solo flying time and 12 500 launches under his belt by December 2012), it's easy to relax.

I signed an indemnity form, and strapped into his two-seater glider (complete with parachutes) in the midday heat. Then we followed the tow plane into the sky. It feels surreal to be towed by another plane but the pilot soon released the cable and we were on our own.

Keith caught a lift off a ridge and climbed to roughly 1 000 metres. We flew over the vast dam and the surrounding tawny countryside, getting an aerial view of the Gariep Dam Forever Resort, the yacht club and hotel. Then Keith followed the Orange River and we drifted downstream above its bends to an island where golfer Gary Player has a ranch.

A regular visitor to the airfield is German Helmut Fischer, who holds the world-record speed for gliding over 1 000 kilometres at 169.7 km/h.

Every gliding season, from about October to April, overseas pilots fly in to Gariep to test their limits and take advantage of the right conditions for this rarefied sport.

Gliding may be a highly controlled sport but it is relatively easy to go for a flight as the passenger of a licensed pilot. High-performance gliders cost several million rands and there are other costs, such as the tow-plane fees. But after floating through the sky, it is easy to understand why glider pilots come back for more – and at Gariep, they are willing to take visitors up for an introductory flight. (For information about other airborne activities you may wish to indulge in, see page 201.)

DESTIJL GARIEP HOTEL

Finding this ultramodern hotel in the Free State heartland was a bonus. Most appealing after 10 hot hours on the road was its infinity pool with a view over the dam. The air-conditioned rooms with queen-size beds and fine linen are minimalist yet stylish. Three huge suites have an open-plan bedroom opening onto a lawn with lounge chairs, a table and panoramic views.

The Mondrian restaurant opens onto an indigenous garden with plants typical of the Karoo. Local dishes like lamb are excellent, as were the pepper steak and pizza.

NOT TOO SHAGGY: SMITHFIELD

Smithfield is in a wool-growing area; its winter festival, BibberChill, includes sheep-shearing and sheepdog competitions. Yet the village has also become an artists' refuge. Art galleries and studios, a fine-felt workshop and a bookstore are among the attractions of this historical town, the third-oldest in the Free State. And it feels like more of an authentic retreat than Clarens, another artists' destination in the province (see page 78).

But Smithfield's appeal is not only aesthetic: not far from the Witteberg Mountains and about 130 kilometres from Gariep Dam, it is partially surrounded by rocky hills and the mountain-biking routes across them are challenging.

The birding in Smithfield is one of the best-kept secrets among twitchers. There are Anglo-Boer War sites nearby; and if you want to know what's on, you can always read the *Smiffie News* or ask acclaimed journalist Carmel Rickard, now resident in Smithfield.

ROCKY MOUNTAIN HIGH

Carmel's partner, Gus Uys, has developed about 50 kilometres of mountain-biking trails in Smithfield, and he took us out one blue morning on one of the easier routes. We rode mostly along a dirt track and then wound up a rocky path on the mountainside, to a ridge with a view over the town. The cycling on this trail allowed us to appreciate the landscape (which is not always the case on technical paths).

Carmel took Zade and another boy for a hike up the mountain while we were riding, and they enjoyed finding animal bones and scented plants, coming back with stones and exuding excitement about their excursion.

Carmel is an informed guide on the bird species in and around Smithfield, which include mountain, vlei and grassland birds. Southern pale chanting goshawks, white-browed sparrow-weavers, three kinds of mousebirds and African harrier-hawks are among the birds in her garden, which she says are attracted by the indigenous plants. Lesser kestrels come to roost around Smithfield from November to March, when they migrate south from Iran.

Paddling on the local dam (six kilometres around the perimeter) and playing a round of golf on the 100-year-old country course – established by British soldiers stationed here during the Anglo-Boer War – are among the outdoor options on offer.

SMITHFIELD BOOKS AND FRESH PAINT GALLERY

Smithfield Books has a fabulous collection of more than 4 000 books and African toys. The bookshop is attached to the Fresh Paint Gallery, run by Greg May, which has an equally compelling range of paintings and collectors' treasures from South Africa and the rest of the continent. Artists like Coral Fourie, Moseokha Klas Thibeletsha and William Pretorius exhibit in the gallery and the gourmet restaurant next to it. The front of the gallery is guarded by two huge blue spotty dogs and the entrance is adorned with mosaic windows.

The four-course meals prepared at the Laughing Likkewaan by chef Francois du Plessis were unexpected in a village like Smithfield.

TRADING PLACES

Vintage enamel signs, such as those for 'Raadsaal' and 'Five Roses Tea', a front stoep with white pillars, bright walls and a large indigenous garden are among the distinctive features of Trading Places Guest House. The rooms are large and uncluttered and it's a peaceful (pet-friendly) place to stay, with a kitchen that can be used by the guests.

Trading Places has four rooms with en suite bathrooms, including one double shower. The third suite, with two bedrooms and a fireplace, is suited to families. This has a shared bathroom and a sitting area with an Edwardian day bed. Fans keep you cool in summer and heaters keep you warm in winter.

IF YOU GO

When to go

The gliding at Gariep Dam is best in summer from about October to April.

Contacts and rates

- The Gariep Dam Nature Reserve consists of the dam and the game sanctuary on its northern shore. Visitors can trace the scenic 165-kilometre route around Lake Gariep, passing through places like Oviston and Bethulie. For more information on local attractions, like the dam wall tour, visit www.gariepdam.com
- Gariep Dam Aviation: introductory gliding flight ◉; web www.gariepdamaviation.com; email info@gariepdamaviation.com
- Gariep Dam Forever Resort gives access to the Free State Yacht Club, where privately owned yachts and dinghies are moored. Waterskiing is also allowed from private speedboats.
- Guided canoeing trips, 5–10 kilometres long, are offered from the resort at ◉ to ◉ per person. Contact Ivan Sinclair, Tel 076 203 9870; email: ivansinclair@vodamail.co.za
- The Gariep Lake Express does boating trips at different times of the day, including sunset tours. Rates per person ◉ to ◉, Tel 051 754 0190
- Destijl Gariep Hotel: standard and superior rooms per person per night ◉; to ◉ depending on the season; per night for a suite ◉. Tel 051 754 0268; web www.destijl.co.za; email reservations@destijl.co.za
- Trading Places: Tel 051 683 0423 or 082 551 3293; web www.tradingplaces2night.co.za; email tradingplaces@iafrica.com

How to get there

Gariep Dam is roughly halfway between Cape Town and Joburg on the N1. Smithfield is about an hour north-east of Gariep Dam along the R701, and a halfway stop on the N6 between Johannesburg and East London.

WESTERN CAPE

19

PRINCE ALBERT & OUDTSHOORN: KAROO TOWNS

The waterfalls and mermaid at Meiringspoort, and the streams and red cliffs of the Swartberg Pass are among the wonders of the Karoo. Across its vast flatness, the Groot Karoo is well known for its arid environment, but crystal streams on the steep Swartberg Pass, pools in nearby Meiringspoort, a perennial water supply in the village of Prince Albert and plants from the Cape Floral Kingdom all make the attractions of the Karoo as wide-ranging as its extreme temperatures.

CLAIRE KEETON

The Swartberg Nature Reserve, which falls between the Klein and Groot Karoo, was proclaimed a UNESCO World Heritage Site in 1997. Prince Albert, which is pivotal to this region, won the Town of the Year competition in the Western Cape in 2012, and it's easy to see why. This historic town celebrated its 250th birthday recently and its original water furrows are preserved along with a working watermill. Cape Dutch and Victorian buildings, 13 of which are national monuments, line the wide streets.

SWARTBERG PASS

An aesthetic and engineering accomplishment, the Swartberg Pass was the last of 16 mountain passes built by master road engineer Thomas Bain in South Africa. 'He built it with the flair and joy of a Da Vinci at the height of his powers,' comments Karoo writer Chris Marais of the 27-kilometre mountain pass, which opened in 1888. Toll fees at the time were 'four pennies per wheel and one penny per animal'. The hand-packed dry-stone walls, built by convicts, are still standing despite the harsh weather.

We appreciated the flowing sweep of this dirt pass, hurtling down its zigzags at dawn on mountain bikes. Our initial intention was to cycle up the pass – which connects Oudtshoorn in the south to Prince Albert in the north – and down again early one morning. But when the temperature rose above 30 °C before sunrise, we changed our plan to ride up to the 1 583-metre summit. Instead we got dropped by car near the top, cycled up for about half an hour

and had the freedom of flying down its switchbacks past intriguing rock formations. We stopped once or twice to scramble up pillars and admire the Cape Fold Belt mountains.

MEIRINGSPOORT

A popular attraction in Meiringspoort, particularly in the Karoo heat, is the Great Waterfall in the gorge. This narrow, 60-metre-high waterfall drops into a dark pool surrounded by rock ledges. Jumping into the cold water from a few metres above, I did not touch the bottom. Children were jumping in from higher and higher parts of the cliff for the thrill. An alluring legend is that of the Karoo mermaid, who lives in the pool with a giant water snake. Reaching the pool entails an easy walk from the road.

Meiringspoort, which links the Klein and Groot Karoo, was the first pass through the Swartberg. Built by a team including Thomas Bain and his father, this road which follows the floor of the gorge, was completed in 1858. But it was susceptible to flooding, precipitating the development of the Swartberg Pass. In 1971 an environmentally-friendly road was opened, which crosses the Groot River 25 times along its 25 kilometres. From Klaarstroom this tarred road (the N12) along the river, which has towering cliffs on either side in Meiringspoort, is a drive worth taking.

The 121 000-hectare Swartberg Nature Reserve has hiking trails, San paintings and different ecosystems, including mountain fynbos and Karoo veld.

BRAKDAKKIE GUEST COTTAGES
The three whitewashed cottages with courtyards – and a plunge pool roughly the size of a large tank for dipping sheep – at Brakdakkie, provide relief from the heat. The interior of our cottage was uncluttered, and included a kitchenette, a big shower and a toilet. An old kid's bicycle and other metal and wood antiques hang on the walls, and succulents thrive in the garden.

KAROO KOMBUIS AND LAZY LIZARD
The Kombuis looks like a traditional Karoo cottage with a stoep, but inside designer high-heel shoes and masks from Venice adorn the walls. The menu at this restaurant, run by three flamboyant former flight attendants, is substantial Karoo fare. When we asked for salad with our lamb, we got the amused reply, 'That's what sheep eat.' Disconcertingly, given what was on the menu, we could see sheep and lambs grazing in the field across the road through the front door. But it's a pretty view. In the morning we had a

ABOVE LEFT: *Cycling up the Swartberg Pass near Prince Albert*
ABOVE RIGHT: *Cooling off at Meiringspoort*

good breakfast at the Lazy Lizard, set in a spacious old house.

SOETKAROO
In scorching afternoon heat, sociable winemaker Susan Perold invited us into her cellar packed with Italian wine-making equipment. After tasting the fortified dessert wine, it would have been easy to lie down on the chilled floor amid the tanks and barrels. The SoetKaroo Wine Estate, in the main road, has only one hectare, where Susan and her husband, Herman, grow, make and bottle their own award-winning wines. Their three wines are only available direct from the cellar.

Olive oil, fresh and dried fruit, and cheese are also produced in Prince Albert.

ACROSS THE PASS
If you cross the Swartberg Pass to

Oudtshoorn, you'll find ostriches, crocodiles and the Cango Caves among the prime tourist attractions. We went crocodile diving at the Cango Wildlife Ranch, ostrich racing at the Cango Ostrich Farm and did the so-called adventure tour in the caves.

Maybe we got the crocs before they had woken up, for this was essentially a tame experience. In a cylindrical cage, one at a time, we were lowered into a clear pool of water where several large crocs lay around. They never took their eyes off us – they were vigilant – but they didn't come close; only one swam around, lazily flicking its tail.

Marianne and her niece and nephew tested the speed of the ostriches. In a pen, one at a time, they mounted a hooded ostrich and, when its hood was removed, the ostrich ran around the paddock while they hung on with varying levels of success. In the end, every novice jockey slides or falls off.

The Cango Caves turned out to be the most exciting Oudtshoorn activity. The caving adventure tour takes you far beyond the main route. We walked through narrow cracks (too small to turn around in), into small grottos with crystals, leopard-crawled down a low tunnel and through other spaces, and at the end climbed up the Devil's Chimney and squeezed through the Devil's Postbox.

If you don't like small spaces, this will feel claustrophobic. If you're neutral, it's a fascinating tour through these dripstone caverns, past stalagmites and helictites. (Read more about caving on page 183.)

IF YOU GO

When to go
Unless you're a heat-seeking missile, like some tourists from the northern hemisphere, avoid these towns in summer. In December, temperatures can rise above 30 °C by 6 am. Winters can also be harsh and frosty, so spring and autumn tend to be the more pleasant seasons to visit.

Contacts and rates
- For hiking permits in the Swartberg Nature Reserve, contact Cape Nature, Oudtshoorn Tel 044 203 6325; web www.patourism.co.za
- Brakdakkie Guest Cottages: from ● per person sharing; for the family cottage ●. To book, Tel 079 185 3554; web www.princealbert.org.za/brakdakkie.htm; email brakdakkie@gmail.com
- Cango Caves Adventure Tour: adults ●; children ●. Tel 044 272 7410; web www.cangocaves.co.za; email reservations@cangocaves.co.za
- Cango Ostrich Farm: entrance, which includes ostrich riding, per person ●. Tel 044 272 4623; web www.cangoostrich.co.za; email cango.ostrich@pixie.co.za
- Cango Wildlife Ranch: entrance per adult ●; per child ●; crocodile diving per person (14 years and older) ●. Tel 044 272 5593; web www.cango.co.za; email info@cango.co.za
- SoetKaroo Wine Estate, Tel 033 541 1768; web www.soetkaroo.co.za; email perold@netactive.co.za

How to get there
You can fly to George Airport and drive an hour or two to get to either destination. The drive from Cape Town is between four and five hours. The Swartberg Pass, which links Prince Albert in the north to Oudtshoorn in the south, is one of South Africa's most striking mountain passes.

20

FOUR RIVERS: KEURBOOMS, KRUIS, STORMS & BLOUKRANS

Rivers evoke a sense of freedom, a chance to float away from landlocked reality to hidden worlds. And within 100 kilometres of each other on the Garden Route are four honey-coloured rivers.

KEURBOOMS RIVER: CANOEING

The Keurbooms River rises in the Langkloof, north of the Tsitsikamma Mountains, and cuts through gorges on its course to the sea. On the ocean side of the Keurbooms River Bridge, the water sprawls into an estuary, while on the mountain side it meanders through forests and past steep cliffs.

The river was an obstacle to the expansion of the Cape Colony in the 19th century before a bridge was built. The first road bridge was washed away by floods in the 1880s, and five years ago, the Keurbooms River mouth washed away Plett's Lookout Beach.

But when Marianne and I went canoeing, the river was flowing serenely and our paddle was more meditative than energetic. We stopped to explore the coves and picnic spots, shaded by keurboom trees, and appreciated the stillness.

In peak season, however, the traffic on the river proliferates with holidaymakers, fishermen, ferries and motorboats up to the four-kilometre buoys, beyond which powerboats are barred.

Canoeists with time on their hands can paddle three kilometres – past the buoy mark along the Whiskey Creek Canoe Trail, to an overnight cabin. (Find out more about canoeing on page 165.)

KRUIS RIVER: WATERFALL ZIP LINING

Three waterfalls make the zip-line tour over the Kruis River, near Storms River, a scenic experience. This activity – essentially a fufi slide with safety equipment, including a harness, helmet, gloves and braking device – goes quicker than the canopy tours. You launch off wide platforms on either side of the gorge and then slide across the river and over the waterfalls.

The longest slide on the Kruis, 50 metres above the river, is 211 metres and you walk a short distance to reach it. The eight slides, nearly 800 metres of line combined, have names like Gravity Junction, the Puff Adder (they found a puff adder there) and Amber Pool.

People can also walk along a suspension bridge to get to an abseiling point above a waterfall. (Find out about other zip-lining locations on page 192.)

STORMS RIVER: BLACKWATER TUBING

Tubing is a relaxed way to explore a river – unless it is flooding, when any river is dangerous – and our trip down the Storms River involved floating, boulder hopping and cliff jumping.

Cape winters, and rivers, are cold, so the best time for tubing is from October to April, not mid-winter, when we did it. Under slate skies we met our guides at Mild 2 Wild Adventures in Storms River village, where we found the thickest wetsuits and booties that fitted us. We got a ride into the forest, and then walked down a muddy path, secured with a rope, to the river. Forests and cliffs converge on the Coke-coloured river gleaming in the gorge.

Tubing on a low river requires some walking – when it is shallow you pull your tube over slippery boulders – but mostly it is effortless. The rapids and chutes were easy at this placid level. However, Storms River can rise rapidly and in March 2000, 13 people died tubing after flooding in a tributary (not with Mild 2 Wild).

On our trip, we flowed gently with the current, past Outeniqua yellowwoods and other giant trees, and stopped halfway for sodas and chocolate.

One of the guides, Rowan Langford, showed us the spots to leap off the cliffs along the way. I jumped off a ledge at the last pool and paddled across to join the others before we headed back to the village.

BLOUKRANS RIVER

The Bloukrans River glinted in the distance as I stood on a platform 216 metres above it, preparing to do a bungee jump. The bungee seems intimidating when you look at it, but I loved it as soon as I was flying and falling.

The Bloukrans River Bungee is on record as the world's highest commercial bridge bungee jump and its famous visitors have included Prince Harry, surfer Kelly Slater and former president Thabo Mbeki.

FIN & CHROME

A neon-pink landmark in the sleepy main street of Storms River, Fin & Chrome is a shrine to Marilyn Monroe and Elvis Presley, filled with photos and memorabilia, and a collection of vintage cars in the Cadillac Shack.

A number plate stating 'Lost in the 50s' expresses the nostalgic mood of the diner, with its black-and-white chequered floor, retro jukebox and rock 'n roll store. Our visit was as practical as it was sentimental – a roaring fire and the desire for coffee – but its fans keep coming back. Like Ronnie's Sex Shop on Route 62, the Fin & Chrome could become an iconic detour.

THYME AND AGAIN

A farm store and deli with tables along the N2, opposite the Keurbooms River turn-off, Thyme & Again is a place where travellers and locals alike drop in for a home-made meal or tea. The spinach-and-feta quiches, chicken-and-mushroom pies, milktart, lemon meringue pie and ginger beer (in season) are recommended.

TAMODI LODGE

Tamodi is one of the most beautiful self-catering lodges we have stayed in. The bedrooms overlook the forests of the Crags, a valley outside Plettenberg Bay, and the Outeniqua Mountains in the distance. The double-volume lounges are huge, with fireplaces, and the rim pool outside has a view over the valley. A wooden deck with a sunken braai pit juts out next to it and the place feels like it is encircled by trees.

Lynne and Owen Johnston have made this an artistic retreat, from the stylish rooms to the driftwood sculptures and elegant screens. Guests can request breakfast, a feast of home-made food.

OPPOSITE: *Marianne paddling down the Keurbooms River*

IF YOU GO

When to go
The Garden Route, like Cape Town, is one of few regions in South Africa with a Mediterranean climate and winter rain. The cold, wet winters are not ideal for outdoor pursuits unless you remain continually active, like with mountain biking. The fynbos and flowers in spring are beautiful. Late summer and autumn are popular seasons in the region for travellers.

Contacts and rates
- Cape Nature Conservation manages the Keurbooms River Nature Reserve. The 14-kilometre Whiskey Creek Canoe Trail takes two days. The hut sleeps up to 10 people, has a deck, braai area and solar showers. Conservation tariff: per person ◉; hut for one to six people per night ◉, per additional person ◉; canoe hire (single or double) per day ◉ (at the entrance). To book, Tel 021 483 0190; web www.capenature.co.za
- To book waterfall zip lining at Tsitsikamma Falls Adventure Park, Tel 042 280 3770 or 082 578 1090; web www.tsitsikammaadventure.co.za; email tsitsikammafalls@lantic.net; per person for the zip-line tour ◉

- The Face Adrenalin bungee jump operates 9 am–5 pm. From ◉ per person to bungee jump; per person for bridge-walking tour ◉. Tel 042 281 1458; web www.faceadrenalin.com; email info@faceadrenalin.com
- Forever Resorts Plettenberg has self-catering chalets (three-star) and eight luxury log cabins at the mouth of the Keurbooms River. The resort has 116 caravan and camping stands with power points, swimming pools and a tennis court. Rates per chalet from ◉ to ◉, depending on the type and season; camping per person per night ◉. For reservations, Tel 012 423 5600; web www.foreverplettenberg.co.za; email info@foreversa.co.za
- Tamodi Lodge: September rates per person sharing a standard suite ◉; October–April per person sharing ◉. Tel Owen Johnston, 082 551 9313; web www.tamodi.co.za; email owen@tamodi.co.za

How to get there
The Garden Route, about three hours' drive along the N2 from Heidelberg in the Western Cape to Port Elizabeth in the Eastern Cape, passes through the Tsitsikamma forest.

21

PLETTENBERG BAY: WHALE BE BACK

A tall fin in the water off Beacon Island Beach, Plettenberg Bay, could be a whale or a great white shark. Sailing in the bay a few years ago, Marianne and I were hoping the fin that came up next to our 14-foot Hobie Cat was attached to a whale – and it turned out to be a Bryde's whale. Whales migrate to South Africa's southern coast every year between July and October. Plett, with its wide, sheltered bay, is one of the best places for whale spotting. We have seen many southern rights, humpbacks and Bryde's whales off Plettenberg Bay from boats and the shore.

Great white sharks are also common, as the seal colony on Robberg Peninsula is a plentiful source of prey. We were not, however, seeking close encounters when we decided to sea-kayak to Robberg Peninsula from Beacon Island Beach.

Sea kayaks are stable and easy to paddle, and we launched into the surf in a double. About 100 metres offshore we waited for our guide, Gareth Weis, from Ocean Blue. We followed him on the paddle (longer than most commercial trips) and we could hear the seals barking and watch their water ballet as we approached the Nek on the Robberg Peninsula. Gareth said a great white, as long as his kayak, once trailed him on a trip with eight clients but fortunately lost interest.

Whales have a long history in the bay – the Beacon Island Hotel is built on the site of an old whaling station. But on that trip we didn't see any. Nevertheless, we had time to admire the open ocean and the bay's dazzlingly white beaches, reminding me of the sentiment in the whaling

OPPOSITE: *Walking on Beacon Island Beach*
ABOVE LEFT: *Walking along the Robberg Peninsula with Plettenberg Bay in the background*
ABOVE RIGHT: *Fountain Hut Bay, where one can overnight on the Robberg Peninsula*

classic *Moby Dick*: 'Whenever I find myself growing grim about the mouth; whenever it is a damp, drizzly November in my soul ... I account it high time to get to sea as soon as I can.' (Find out more about sea kayaking on page 158.)

A STROLL ON SEAL MOUNTAIN

Take the time to walk the longest of the three circular routes around Robberg (about 10 kilometres), and you will have a chance to appreciate its beauty and history. We set out on the side of the headland that overlooks Robberg Beach and Plettenberg Bay, walking to the point that extends nearly four kilometres into the Indian Ocean, before returning about four hours later to the

ABOVE: *Whales spotted from the Robberg Peninsula*
LEFT: *Marianne's husband and niece take a beach stroll at Robberg*

car park. The route has information boards about the marine life, geology – Robberg has remarkable pebbled rock formations – and sites of historical significance here.

We walked along a winding path and, nearing the Gap, where the peninsula narrows to 160 metres, we could hear the seal colony below. The Cape fur seal colony, after which Robberg is named (Afrikaans for Seal Mountain), was wiped out at the turn of the last century and re-established in the mid-1990s.

Past the seals, the path winds down to shelves of rock next to pounding waves. The route is safe at low tide, but hikers must watch out for freak waves, which have swept people away. (The Robberg Point shack was also washed away by such a wave.)

We walked past large rock pools up a steeper section. The path steers along a narrow ridge, where the more exposed sections are protected by a wooden boardwalk and stairs. From the hill, you descend to a sandy beach, where the Robberg Fountain Hut (which sleeps eight people) is located, with a spectacular view over the beach to the attached island, and the ocean. An hourglass-shaped sandbank with waves on both sides (called a tombolo) links the island, with its fossil dunes, to the peninsula. From the beach you climb the path back to the car park.

FISH AND CHIPS, HOT CROISSANTS

The Plettenberg Bay Ski-Boat Association has a clubhouse on Beacon Island Beach, which serves only fish caught that morning. If you arrive too late, you miss out. We found a vacant table and ate the best fish I've ever tasted, with crisp chips and servings so generous we struggled to finish them.

In town, Le Fournil de Plett, a bakery and cafe run by a Frenchwoman, Florence Chabanel, and South African Jen Hops, has outstanding croissants and cappuccinos, and serves meals.

ON THE WATER

We stayed in Beau Rivage, a functional townhouse complex on the lagoon in the Piesang Valley, a 10-minute walk from Robberg Beach. Our three-room house on the water provided comfortable and safe self-catering accommodation, with an en suite bedroom outside.

IF YOU GO

When to go
Summer holidays see an enormous influx of tourists into Plettenberg Bay and the surrounds from all over the country, as the weather is brilliant. Cooler, wet winters may at times limit enjoyment of outdoor activities, depending on your sensibilities.

Contacts and rates
- Ocean Blue: sea kayaking per person ▪. Tel 044 533 5083 or 083 701 3583; web www.oceanadventures.co.za; email info@oceanadventures.co.za
- Beau Rivage: No. 48 (where we stayed) is available from ▪ a night upwards. Tel 082 494 9416; web www.findersseekers.co.za/plett.php; email info@findersseekers.co.za

How to get there
Sedgefield and Plett are around five and a half hours from Cape Town along the gorgeous coastal N2 highway. George Airport serves most major national centres.

22

GREATER TSITSIKAMMA: NOETZIE,
NATURE'S VALLEY, CLOUDS AND SNAKES

Nature's Valley, in the Tsitsikamma National Park, and nearby Noetzie, are like Peter Pan's Neverland, with dreamy beaches, lagoons, coves and castles offering an escape from everyday life. Unlike the nearby holiday towns of Plettenberg Bay and Knysna, they are relatively untouched by development.

Nature's Valley has the distinction of being a holiday village inside a park, and the Otter Trail, through the park, ends here. The village, which has only about a hundred permanent residents, was established at the Groot River mouth, alongside the estuary. To reach it, we wound down the steep pass towards the ocean, with the mist rising off the forest canopy and mountains behind us.

NATURE'S VALLEY TO KEURBOOMS

We did a four-hour, 12-kilometre hike from Nature's Valley to Keurbooms River mouth with Galeo Saintz, a conservationist who offers guided walks. It was out of season and we didn't see a single other person.

At dawn we parked in front of the tea shop on the west side – Nature's Valley has only one store and restaurant – and walked onto the beach. Elongated shadows stretched ahead of us on the white sand as we followed the trail into the forest. From the ridge, we dropped down to the shore again and walked along rocks and sand, and back into the forest.

OPPOSITE AND ABOVE: *Claire and Marianne walking from Nature's Valley to Keurbooms Beach* PIC: GALEO SAINTZ

We hiked past soaring Arch Rock and onto a little curved beach on the Salt River Estuary, where we crossed a wide river. Prehistoric insects have been discovered here. From the cove, we climbed to an official lookout point – this trail has myriad viewpoints – where you can see east and west for miles along the coast.

Keurbooms marked the end of our walk. Here we walked up a flight of stairs into another semi-deserted, out-of-season village. Even the landmark Ristorante Enrico was closed.

NOETZIE

This secluded cove near Plettenberg Bay is known for its private castles (eight castles tower over Noetzie – one of them abandoned); and there is a scattering of houses, mostly in the forest bordering the Sinclair Nature Reserve. The white beach and warm lagoon lead into the Noetzie River, one of the country's cleanest.

Enjoying the view from Harkerville Forest

We spent hours swimming in the lagoon, canoeing up the river (where we saw a green snake) and playing in the ocean during a weekend I spent there with my son and his friends. On a *Sunday Times* Explorer trip in 2010, I also spent a fabulous night in Noetzie – that time at Lindsay Castle, which has stone turrets, arched doors and windows, and a great big round table.

HARKERVILLE TRAILS

Between Plett and Knysna is Harkerville Forest, which has some of the best mountain-biking routes in the country, day walks and horse paths.

At the Garden of Eden you enter the forest and find a choice of yellow, blue, green and red circular cycle routes, colour-coded by distance (12, 14, 15 and 24 kilometres), not severity. You can ride on single-track routes under the tall trees, including hard pears and stinkwoods, and through coastal fynbos.

Among our stops were the Kranshoek viewpoint and picnic site. Here you look down on beaches far below, offshore rock formations and giant waves crashing against the rocks. From Kranshoek we returned along the hilly gravel road to the Kranshoek Road gate.

Keen hikers can do the Kranshoek day walk (nine kilometres) through the forest or follow the two-day

Harkerville Coast Hiking Trail, which has two huts along the way.

Horse riders can follow their own marked trails through the forest.

TSITSIKAMMA CANOPY TOUR

The Tsitsikamma Canopy Tour is the oldest of South Africa's canopy tours. Some of the trees on this route are 700 years old.

On the tour through the forest canopy, you wear a body harness to enable you to glide as swiftly as you choose through the treetops. You travel along a steel cable about 30 metres above the ground and slide from one platform to another. Eleven platforms have been constructed in hard pear trees and the longest slide is 96 metres. The tour starts from Storms River Village; bookings are essential.

LAWNWOOD SNAKE SANCTUARY

When Michael Caithness attempted to give his python, Axel, a kiss, the 3.5-metre snake sank 70 or so razor-sharp teeth into his face and started wrapping itself around his body. His wife, Emily, then pregnant, and their assistants rescued him. The couple started Lawnwood 11 years ago, when Michael's snake collection grew too large for their home.

Eight years later, Axel, the sleek offspring of a Burmese python mom and African rock python dad, is still a star at the Lawnwood Snake Sanctuary, near Plettenberg Bay. He hangs out with his mates, a dozen or so pythons, boa constrictors and anacondas, in three large enclosures.

Axel's slinky looks caught Marianne's eye and she suggested I pick him up for a photo. That was before we had heard about Michael's narrow escape. We both like handling non-venomous snakes and felt safe enough, but after that story I was unwilling to get too close to Axel. The expression 'heads or tails' took on a new spin: when we held an albino python, Marianne got the head and I got the tail.

What's special about this sanctuary is that guests are allowed to hold snakes under supervision and there are 25 indigenous snakes in a deep, open pit. About 50 indigenous and exotic snakes are housed in a large dome; in total they keep about 100 snakes – non-venomous, semi-venomous and venomous.

Among the other reptiles at the sanctuary are crocodiles and African monitor lizards, which can lock onto prey with their jaws. On the one-hour tour, you learn about what to do if you encounter a snake. Standing still until it slithers away is usually the safest option.

SEDGEFIELD FROM THE AIR
You're never too old for adventure. Tandem paragliding pilot Jan Minnaar once took a woman for her first flight on her 65th birthday from the top of the ridge that overlooks Sedgefield. Despite living for decades in this pretty town surrounded by water – the Indian Ocean, Swartvlei Estuary and coastal lakes – she had never seen it from above. A flight giving her a true aerial view of Sedgefield, with the experienced crew of Cloudbase Paragliding, was her present.

Within minutes of my saying hello to this crew, Khobi Minnaar, an internationally qualified competition paraglider, had helped me into the tandem paragliding harness and found a helmet to fit. We had an easy take-off, running for only a few steps before the paraglider started to lift off, and we were airborne. Once we were in the sky, Jan found thermals to lift us high above the forested ridge. This gave me a unique perspective on this coastal hideaway, with its dunes covered in fynbos and extensive lakes.

Floating above the town, I felt relaxed, peaceful and safe. And our landing back on the ridge was so smooth it felt like stepping off a stool onto the floor.

Microlighting is fun but noisy. So, if you've dreamt of flying, paragliding is one of the purest ways to get your head in the clouds. (Find out more about paragliding on page 201.)

GARDEN ROUTE: FINE DINING
After cranking up our appetites on the Harkerville trails, we were ready for a three-course meal at the Emily Moon restaurant, overlooking the Bitou River and wetlands, on the outskirts of Plettenberg Bay. The food served at this wine-tasting evening was outstanding.

The critically acclaimed Ile de Pain (Island of Bread) bakery and bistro in nearby Knysna, on Thesen Island, is another memorable eatery. This bistro has published its own recipe book, and Marianne, a talented cook, has been impressed by the results.

At the Bramon Wine Estate you can taste the wines at the restaurant, on the edge of the vineyards, along with local cheeses, home-made bread and dishes from a tapas-style menu.

Zinzi, a Hunter Hotels restaurant

outside Knysna, is exceptional. Every detail, from the mud chandeliers to the custom-made furniture, enhances the atmosphere, and the food was excellent.

TREETOPS AND LILIES

The exquisite Tsala Treetop Lodge, about an hour by road from Storms River, is designed to blend into the indigenous forest. What makes it special are the treetop suites on stilts, reached by an elevated wooden walkway. Floor-to-ceiling glass in the suites gives you a sense of being encircled by nature.

Lily Pond Country Lodge is a serene establishment just seven kilometres from Nature's Valley. Three lily ponds and a deck are the focus of the garden, which is surrounded by indigenous forest in a private nature reserve.

Hikers' Cabin is a self-catering cottage near Nature's Valley that sleeps 12.

IF YOU GO

When to go
This green, lush and largely mild region (most of the year) means one can take advantage of most outdoor sports, although mid-winter can be cold and wet.

Contacts and rates
- Nature's Valley to Keurbooms Walk: rates from ◉ per person, depending on numbers. Tel 082 888 8181; web www.walkandnature.com
- Harkerville trails: all four trails start and finish at the Garden of Eden, on the N2, where permits must be obtained. Garden of Eden, Tel 044 532 7793; open 7.30 am–4 pm, Monday to Friday. Alternatively, get a permit ◉ at the Kranshoek Road gate. You must carry your permit on the trails. Some routes may be closed after rain. It's safe to drink the water from the rooibos-coloured streams in the forest. To book for the hiking trails, contact the Knysna Forestry Office, Tel 044 382 5863.
- Tsitsikamma Canopy Tours: rate per person for two hours ◉; Tel 042 281 1836 or 027 42 281 1836; web www.tsitsikammacanopytour.co.za; email adventure@gardenroute.co.za
- Outeniqua Bike Hire (for Harkerville trails), from the legendary Kevin Evans biking family.

Rates per person ◉. Tel 044 532 7644 or 083 252 7997; email bikesshop@mweb.co.za
- Lawnwood Snake Sanctuary: open daily 9 am–5 pm. Entry fee: ◉ (teenagers and children pay less). For more information, Tel 044 534 8056 or 082 667 6588; email lawnwood@polka.co.za
- Cloudbase Paragliding: per person ◉. Tel 044 877 1414 or 082 777 8474; email jan@cloudbase-paragliding.co.za
- Bookings are recommended for Bramon Wine Estate. For details, Tel 044 534 8007 or 073 833 8183; web www.bramonwines.co.za; email restaurant@bramonwines.co.za
- Lily Pond Country Lodge: rates from ◉ to ◉ off season; higher in season (October–April). Tel 044 534 8767 or 082 746 8782; web www.lilypond.co.za; email info@lilypond.co.za
- Hikers' Cabin: per night for four people ◉; per additional person ◉. Tel 082 448 7953; web www.hikerscabin.co.za; email lucinda@farmerschoice.co.za

How to get there
Look out for turn-offs from the beautiful Garden Route N2 highway, which acts as the spine for all of these destinations. You can fly to nearby George Airport and rent a car from there.

23

MOSSEL BAY: PREDATOR PLAY TIME

The sharks are on safari but the humans don't impress them much. Imagine watching a lion hunt when you're in the hooves of an impala. That's how it feels to be submerged in the sea when a four-metre great white shark lunges at you, jaws open, even though you're protected by the steel bars of a cage. But most of the time, the sharks just glide past, barely turning their heads to look at the people squashed in the cage in wetsuits. One gets the feeling that the trapped human beings in the cage aren't worth a second glance.

From my perspective, the ocean's top predators are among the natural wonders of the world and cage diving in Mossel Bay – along with Gansbaai, further west – is an extraordinary experience. But cage diving is controversial, particularly near swimming beaches, where attacks on surfers and swimmers are a concern. On the other hand, cage diving raises awareness about these magnificent endangered predators and supports shark conservation and research.

SHARK DIVING AND VIEWING

You can go cage diving without being a qualified diver, or you can view the sharks from the deck of a boat. Cage diving involves pulling yourself down to the floor of a floating cage and holding your breath. The cage is attached to the boat and has enough space above the surface to allow you to stand up and breathe easily.

Seal Island, about a kilometre from the shore of Mossel Bay, is a hunting ground for great white sharks, and tourists have about an 80 per cent chance of spotting them on a cage-

ABOVE: *Cage diving among great white sharks in Mossel Bay*

diving or shark-viewing trip. The boat ride from Mossel Bay Harbour is about 10 minutes; the water temperature ranges from 15 to 24 °C; wetsuits are provided.

Marianne and I went out with White Shark Africa – the only cage-diving operator on the Garden Route.

The crew dropped anchor near the island, which is crammed with barking Cape fur seals. Not long after chumming the water (throwing out a mix of fish oil, minced sardine and tuna) and a bait line with a tuna head, the great whites glided up to the boat.

They typically approached from below, close to the bars of the cage, and one huge adult bumped it and made the divers shake, literally and figuratively. We felt a sense of wonder watching the sharks up close.

If you prefer to stay dry, viewing sharks from a platform above the cabin or from the deck of the *Shark Warrior* is an excellent alternative.

SHARK DIVING UNLIMITED

In Gansbaai, near Hermanus, our group saw 13 sharks from the cage and the boat in less than two hours. Even my untrained eye could identify some of the distinguishing features in terms of size, shades of grey and scars on the dorsal fins of the *Carcharodon carcharias*.

The concentration of great whites near Dyer Island's seal colony, about 20 minutes' boat ride from the shore, is astounding, and so is their stealth: one minute, there's no shark at the stern; the next minute, two are slicing through the water, swiftly and benignly.

Shark Diving Unlimited supports scientific research. It assisted a DNA project in which 33 sharks were photographically identified and from which DNA tissue samples were collected.

The owner of the organisation,

Michael Rutzen, nicknamed Sharkman, has been following great whites for nearly 20 years and is one of a few researchers who swim among them without the protection of a cage.

TO DIVE OR NOT TO DIVE

Sharks die when their fins are cut off, and humans are annihilating them. Finned sharks sink unseen to the seabed to die. An estimated 150 million sharks are killed every year, warns White Shark Africa, and these sharks face the threat of extinction unless conservation becomes a priority.

Cage diving allows people the chance to appreciate the power of sharks in their element and understand why they are a vital link in the ocean's food chain.

Opponents of cage diving and chumming say the activity disturbs the animals' natural behaviour and teaches them to associate humans with food. But shark experts, like Ryan Johnson from Oceans Research, accept shark diving as a compromise that promotes the awareness of the species, helps to collect data and raises funds for shark research. (Find out more about cage diving on page 162.)

SLEEPING IN A 'LIGHTHOUSE'

The Point Village Hotel has spacious self-catering apartments and en suite rooms in the popular tourist area of Mossel Bay, the Point. The apartment we shared had a sunny, open-plan kitchen/living room with a balcony and two comfortable bedrooms. The front of the Point Village Hotel resembles a red lighthouse (it is not far from the real lighthouse on the Point). The interior has original African artworks and mosaics, which brighten up the space.

Request an apartment on the street side overlooking the sea.

COFFEE AND MOJITOS

The smell of baking infuses D'Bistro coffee shop in Mossel Bay, which is one of the best places to eat out.

The food is made with attention to detail and our home-baked croissants, home-made jam and cappuccinos were just right. The coffee shop/deli also has delicacies and gifts for sale.

Delfino's restaurant on the Point, overlooking the sea, is well located for sundowners.

Cafe Havana is a good meeting spot for cocktails and snacks. The decor of this old house with large balconies conjures up a Latin vibe.

IF YOU GO

When to go
Mossel Bay Tourism reckons that the town gets 300 days of sunshine a year, which makes it a great place for outdoor activities; and the bay is usually calm, which is ideal for shark diving and other ocean pursuits.

Contacts and rates
- White Shark Africa: per person ● (rate for South African residents). You get a voucher for a free trip if you don't see any sharks when you go out on the two- to four-hour boat ride. Tel 044 691 3796 or 082 455 2438; web www.sharkafrica.co.za; email sharkafrica@mweb.co.za
- Point Village Hotel: per person sharing ●; single per room ●; double/twin rate per room ●. Tel 044 690 3156; web www.pointvillagehotel.co.za; email stay@pointvillagehotel.co.za

How to get there
Mossel Bay is halfway between Cape Town and Port Elizabeth, roughly 400 kilometres from either city.

24 CEDERBERG & GROOT WINTERHOEK:
ROCK 'N JOL

Sculpted red sandstone formations in the Cederberg wilderness area in the Western Cape resemble desert rock, but an abundance of rooibos-coloured streams and rock pools set this mountainous valley apart as an oasis for hikers, rock climbers and families just looking for a getaway. At night the stars in the unpolluted sky dazzle as brightly as over the Namib Desert, making it a premier star-gazing destination.

Cederberg rock is textured and solid: it makes you want to touch it and scramble up the carved boulders, and to explore the cracks and caves along the cliffs, whether you're a climber or a child.

For nearly 20 years, I've been visiting the 172 000-hectare conservancy of the Cederberg and every time I am awestruck by its beauty. Marianne felt the same way when we went on our first trip: impressed not only by the rock climbing but by its ancient magic. And since he was little, my son has loved the place.

My favourite base is Sanddrif, a nature resort at the base of the Wolfberg Cracks and on the banks of the Dwars River. I've also camped wild in the fynbos below Tafelberg Mountain after climbing it, and at an established campsite at Rocklands.

IN THE JAWS OF THE WOLF

The Maltese Cross, a sandstone pillar that resembles the symbol, the Wolfberg Cracks and Maalgat Pool are popular day walks from Sanddrif, and the cracks and the cross are excellent traditional climbing crags. The short Sanddrif Crag, near the resort, has been bolted for sport climbing.

Marianne and I climbed a short crack up the Maltese Cross – reminding me of a climb I did in the desert in Utah, which also has dramatic carved-out rock towers – and we did routes inside the Wolfberg Cracks. Classic, clean lines have been opened here and on the faces by bold, talented climbers, like the late David Davies. (For more on rock climbing, see page 178.)

The hikes up to the Maltese Cross and Wolfberg Cracks and Arch, which wind through astonishing formations and across streams, are worth the effort.

Walking along the Dwars River through the Valley of the Red Gods, which has rocky coves and stretches of wide sandy beaches, to Maalgat is an easy meander and the clear water of the pool is great for swimming in summer, but chilly at other times. Maalgat has high jumps from its cliffs.

Another short hike, recommended by Sanddrif (we haven't done it yet), is the trail to the Stadsaal Caves, where you can see San paintings.

The hike up to Tafelberg Mountain is longer and less clearly marked, but has abundant flowers alongside the path in spring. Overnight hiking in the Cederberg – home to the endangered Clanwilliam cedar tree – and sleeping under the stars are truly wild experiences, but you need a permit.

Rocklands, further north, is well known for bouldering (gymnastic climbing with mats for protection – a fun activity). Rocklands attracts international sport climbers. (Read more about bouldering on page 180.)

Mountain bikers can also test their skills on trails like Lot's Wife – but the climbing is so compelling we didn't get to riding. The area also has 4x4 trails to explore.

STARGAZING

The Cederberg Observatory, run by amateur astronomers, got its own dome about 30 years ago after being established in the early 1980s. On Saturday nights, it is open to visitors for about two hours, and one of its astronomers presents a slideshow on the skies, before unveiling the edges of the universe through a telescope. You can observe faraway galaxies, Jupiter's moons, globular clusters and other wondrous bright sights.

The viewing is closed at full moon and depends on the weather.

WINE TASTING

The Cederberg Private Cellar produces fine wines. It has won a range of awards (including the Veritas Double Gold medal) and *Platter's South African Wine Guide* also gives its whites and reds many star ratings. At about 1 000 metres above sea level, this winery has the highest vineyards in the Western Cape, enabling it to harvest a month later than normal.

FLY PORTERVILLE

Porterville, in the 19 000-hectare Groot Winterhoek conservancy, close to the Cederberg, has world-class paragliding, with annual competitions held from the Dasklip Pass along the ridge. The landowner forbids commercial flying but tandem flights can be arranged in advance through the Fly Porterville club. You can reciprocate with beers and pizza. I've made two gentle flights off the pass – one with a friend when four months pregnant, and another with a pilot from Birdmen Paragliding.

Boulders, mountain fynbos and streams characterise the wilderness area of the Groot Winterhoek at the top of the mountain. The reserve has nine hiking trails from 5 to 14 kilometres in length, and there are San

paintings hidden among the rocks en route. Sandstone boulders, eroded into curious shapes, dominate this landscape. The Groot Winterhoek is also known for its disas: 135 out of 160 species of these orchids are found in this region.

ACCOMMODATION
Sanddrif

Sanddrif Holiday Resort is an outdoor paradise – a great escape from city life and excellent for children. The willowy, green campsite on a meadow next to the river has braai spots, electricity and two ablution blocks. When planning, check if school groups are camping at Sanddrif and try to visit out of school holidays if you want undiluted peace.

The Cederberg feels remote and has limited cellphone reception (there is none at Sanddrif) and no formal shops. We stocked up at Citrusdal; the farm shop had a few essentials as well as home-made options, such as koeksisters. We stayed at Dollie Se Huis, a spacious thatched cottage with two bedrooms, a verandah, an outdoor braai area and a huge indoor fireplace.

Cedar Peak

Self-catering accommodation at Cedar Peak Farm, in the Groot Winterhoek, is remote and pet friendly.

Rooibos Cottage and the original Blomhof farmhouse both have stunning views of the mountains and over the Olifants River Valley.

The wide porches (both equipped with hammocks), French doors, Cape cottage furniture, bamboo ceilings and whitewashed walls make the cottage and farmhouse attractive places to stay.

Laatson

A collection of simple cottages set under trees on a farmer's land, close to the village of Porterville, make Laatson popular with paragliders and families.

IF YOU GO

When to go
Spring and autumn are perfect seasons to visit the Cederberg and Groot Winterhoek, but in the shade (for example, climbing in the Wolfberg Cracks) it can get cold, so be prepared. In summer this area gets hot, but rivers (like the Dwars at Sanddrif) with sandy, shady banks and pools like Maalgat, make the heat tolerable. If you want the silence of the wilderness, avoid the school holidays.

Contacts and rates
- Cape Nature: day hike permits per adult ◉; for children (2–13), permits cost less. Tel 086 122 7362/8831 (0861CapeNature) 086122 7362 8873; www.capenature.co.za; or contact Sanddrif (details below)
- Groot Winterhoek Wilderness Area, Cape Nature. Tel 022 931 2860 or 086 122 7362/8873 (0861CapeNature); web www.capenature.co.za
- Porterville Tourism: Tel 022 931 3732; web www.portervilletourism.co.za; email info@portervilletourism.co.za
- For stargazing, email malcolm@icegroup.co.za (Afrikaans) or Chris at camkit@mweb.co.za (English); web www.cederbergobs.org.za
- Cederberg Private Cellar: wine tasting per person ◉; open Monday to Saturday, 8.30 am–noon and 2 pm–4 pm www.cederbergwine.com
- Fly Porterville: contact Coral Benn, Tel 022 931 3567; web www.flyporterville.info;

email coral@flysa.net
- Birdmen Paragliding: Tel 021 557 8144 or 082 658 6710; web www.birdmen.co.za; email birdmen@xsinet.co.za
- Sanddrif: cottages for four people per cottage ◉ and per additional person ◉; camping for four people per site ◉ and a small fee per additional person. Tel 027 482 2825; web www.cederberg.co.za/sanddrif.html; email sanddrif@cederbergwine.com
- Cedar Peak: Rooibos Cottage per night ◉; Blomhof farmhouse per night (up to four adults and two children) ◉; per additional adult ◉; per additional child ◉. Tel 021 438 7702; bookings through www.budget-getaways.co.za; for more information, www.cedarpeak.co.za
- Laatson: chalets for two people per night ◉ and per additional person ◉. Tel 022 931 2339; web www.laatson.co.za; email bookings@22watervalle.co.za

How to get there
The Cederberg is three hours easy driving from Cape Town International Airport – you take the N7 off the N1 highway. After Citrusdal, turn off the N7 at the Algeria/Cederberg sign. The last hour or so of driving into the Cederberg Conservancy is on dirt road over the Uitkyk Pass. The Groot Winterhoek is even closer. To reach the Groot Winterhoek, you go up Dasklip Pass, near Porterville.

25

MONTAGU & SIMONSKLOOF: THE FULL MONTY

WESTERN CAPE

Rock spires, pyramids and the ridges of the Langeberg Mountains encircle Montagu, an enchanting village with rivers running through it. On the Klein Karoo's Route 62, Montagu is one of South Africa's best sport climbing and outdoor destinations.

Its natural wonders, including hot mineral springs, are only part of Montagu's charms. Fine food and wine abound in Montagu, which is near to the orchards and vineyards of the Robertson Valley. Artists and photographers converge on the village, attracted by the landscape, and writers and musicians drop in on its festivals. A film crew from Bollywood came to Montagu in 2012 to film a climbing stunt scene. Historical buildings, which have outlasted repeated floods (Montagu is susceptible to flooding; the last one was in 2012) add to the appeal of this town founded in 1851. Old Cape Dutch houses are among the 14 national monuments that line Long Street, which reportedly has the most national monuments in a single street in South Africa.

When you approach Montagu from Cape Town via the Cogmanskloof Pass – driving through an arched tunnel blasted in the rock by famed road engineer Thomas Bain in 1899 – you feel like you're entering another era. Montagu seems to move at a gentle pace, not unlike

OPPOSITE: *Climbing on Cogman's Buttress outside Montagu*
ABOVE LEFT: *Horse riding in the fynbos outside Montagu*
ABOVE RIGHT: *Kloofing and adventure walking in Simonskloof*

the tortoises protected in this village by FOOT (Friends of Our Tortoises). Besides the old-timers who have lived here forever, Montagu's population now includes lifestyle migrants from across the country who have fallen under its spell.

SIMONSKLOOF AND NUY RIVER GORGE

The Nuy River Gorge, where leopard roam, is remote and, like Simonskloof Mountain Retreat, 50 kilometres from Montagu, it is a wilderness where mountain fynbos and succulent Karoo biospheres meet.

At Simonskloof you hear only silence or wind when you sit around a fire at night or look at the stars from your bed. This is a place to get away from the world. Jurgen Wohlfarter, an eco-friendly hippy who runs this down-to-earth organic farm – the type of place where Sacred Sweat Lodge ceremonies are held – has infused the retreat with soul and a respect for the environment.

When baboons once came too close, Jurgen says he got them off his territory by barking at them. Simonskloof is about back-to-nature communication – cellphones don't work here. Jurgen and his partner have candle-lit dinners every night, he says, describing how he is content to live off the grid with solar and candle power.

But the couple and his border collies are not alone: Simonskloof is a magnet for WWOOFers (Willing Workers On Organic Farms).

Kloofing in the Nuy River Gorge, which requires abseiling down to the river, boulder hopping and hiking, is the most popular activity among guests. The golden-red overhanging walls are impressive; trees along the banks (unfortunately also alien species) offer shade and the tawny-coloured river has pools.

Our kloofing day with Jurgen was relaxed and went quickly – but we didn't need any instruction abseiling – and we saw a mountain tortoise on our way back to the cottage where we were staying.

The cottages are rustic and have beautiful views. The Faraway Cottage had a cold bath in the fynbos with a view; the shower is heated by solar panels. The campsites, set next to a river and boulders, have ablutions and a giant oak for shelter.

Simonskloof won the award for Best Adventure, Outdoor and/ or Ecotourism Business in the Cape

ABOVE AND OPPOSITE: *Kloofing and adventure walking in Simonskloof*

Winelands District Municipality Mayoral Tourism Awards, 2012.

COGMAN'S BUTTRESS, LEGO LAND, THE STEEPLE AND BADSKLOOF

Montagu has every grade of climbs from easy beginner to technically very hard and, along with Waterval Boven, the best range of bolted routes in the country among the 450 listed. No wonder Montagu attracts the best climbers in the world; and legendary South African climbers, like Cape Town's Ed February, have set up a weekend base here.

Climbing more than 150 metres to the top of Cogman's Buttress with a friend when my son was still a toddler (and safely on the ground) gave me a sense of freedom.

On a second trip with Marianne at Easter 2013, we decided to do this lofty route again – appropriately called Another Day in Paradise – and I found it as much fun the second time round. As a bonus, you get a peerless view of Montagu from the summit.

The Steeple and Lego Land are quick-access crags; the Steeple has a small family-friendly beach.

The 12-kilometre Cogmanskloof hike up the mountainside to the 690-metre summit is another way to experience this vista. You can also explore the fort built by the British during the Anglo-Boer War, a national monument, above the tunnel, and see Cogmanskloof Pass, which links Montagu to Ashton.

Climbing off the beach at Badkloof, another great crag in Montagu, is easy. Kids can play in the sand or splash in the Kingna River while adults play on the rock, much of it overhanging. We did some classic routes on the Waterworld Crag.

A 2.2-kilometre trail along the river and reeds through Badkloof links the hot springs with the Ou Meul in town.

De Bos Guest Farm is a popular backpackers and camping spot for climbers, who congregate here on weekends and holidays, and get discounts.

RIDING HORSES AND BIKES

Celebrity endurance rider Petrus van der Merwe has a farm outside Montagu (Groenpunt Equestrian Centre) where he trains long-distance riders, and offers horse riding. His three daughters are Springbok endurance riders and Janine led our ride. She must have found it tedious plodding along with amateurs. Marianne and I were hoping to trot and canter but most of it was restricted to walking through the fynbos with some rocky terrain. First-time rider Muneeba Abrahams, from Landsdowne in Cape Town, said she found the ride exhilarating and scary.

From horses we turned our attention to bike riding and, because of persistent rain, which is unusual, we went for a sightseeing cycle along the flat roads of Montagu past its monuments and the Leidam, which has 18 species of birds and a hide for bird spotting.

RAMBLING ROSE, MO & ROSE, THOMAS BAIN PUB

The remarkable number of places to eat and drink in Montagu far exceeds its size. The Rambling Rose coffee shop/deli is one of the newest additions and its coffee (from Origins in Cape Town) is the finest in Montagu. The breakfast menu was exceptional, and we got fresh bread and gourmet cheeses here for our lunches on the mountains.

Die Kloof Padstall, a farm stall near the bridge, is another good place for provisions; it has pancakes on the menu and a children's playground.

After one long day out, we met the experienced climbing guides Justin and Riki Lawson at the Thomas Bain Pub/Prestons Restaurant in town, opposite another recommended eatery and the backpackers, The Mystic Tin. This good-natured couple dreamt of a place in Montagu when they worked in the IT industry in London and now they are living their dream with their toddler son. They

BELOW: *Exploring Montagu by bicycle*

guide, own and run South Africa's biggest climbing forum, Climb ZA, and are endlessly enthusiastic. We joined them one evening at the wine bistro, the Mo & Rose at Soekershof, about half an hour out of Montagu. Near Robertson, the Mo & Rose has a guest house, serves fine food in the restaurant and has unusual indigenous gardens to wander around after (over)eating.

AASVOELKRANS

Of all the places I've stayed, Aasvoelkrans in Montagu is one of my most memorable and I want to go back. It's beautifully designed and decorated by resident painter Jeanne Alston and her husband. What I liked most was the view of the mountains in the distance and, in front of my room, the Arabian horses wandering around the paddocks in the morning mist, and the flowers everywhere. This six-acre farm with spacious garden rooms is a special place.

The hostess has a reputation for being temperamental. She writes, for example, on her website that 'all baked goods (freshly baked bread, strawberry scones, bran muffins, cinnamon and apple crumpets) are produced based upon your hostess's mood'. Our breakfasts were great and she was gracious.

In the early morning, the couple would go hiking for three hours on the mountain in preparation for the Camino De Santiago in Spain, a pilgrimage they have done twice. Aasvoelkrans has its own short trail on the mountain.

IF YOU GO

When to go
Montagu has sunny weather for much of the year, making it a perfect outdoor destination. The summers get very hot and the winters cold (with snow on the high mountains) but it is an all-year-round destination.

Contacts and rates
- Montagu Climbing: trips start at ▪ for two hours for beginners, equipment provided. Tel Justin Lawson 023 614 3193 or 082 696 4067; web www.montaguclimbing.com/www.climbing.co.za; email Justin@climbing.co.za
- De Bos Guest Farm: Rates for climbers range upwards per night for camping from ▪ to ▪ for en suite rooms. The options include the Backpackers' Barn, Courtyard, Garden Cottage and Bungalows. Tel 023 614 2532; web www.debos.co.za; email: info@debos.co.za
- Simonskloof and Nuy River Gorge: kloofing trips per day, including lunch ▪; self-catering cottages start at ▪ for two people; camping per person per night ▪. Tel Jurgen Wohlfarter 023 614 1895; web www.simonskloof.com; email: info@simonskloof.com
- Aasvoelkrans: per person per night ▪. Tel 023 61 41228; web www.aasvoelkrans.co.za; email jeanne@aasvoelkrans.co.za
- Bike and helmet rental from Die Kuns Kas: per hour ▪; more for full day. Tel 082 457 0319
- Horse riding: per person for two hours ▪. Tel 023 614 2255 or 082 938 5193

How to get there
Montagu doesn't demand a pilgrimage to appreciate its beauty. It is about a two-hour drive from Cape Town along the N1 through the Huguenot Tunnel; Simonskloof is 50 kilometres outside of Montagu.

26

CAPE TOWN: TABLE MANNERS

Everyone knows Table Mountain. Capetonians live in its shadow; tourists take the cableway to the top; hikers tramp through its fynbos; and climbers hang off its sandstone cliffs. It's a World Heritage Site, one of the Seven Wonders of Nature and an adventure playground. The Cape Peninsula, with Cape Point at its tip, is almost as famous, and it offers spectacular road cycling, horse riding, hiking in nature reserves and child-friendly beaches along the way.

TABLE MOUNTAIN ROCKS

Despite having climbed on Table Mountain for years, Marianne and I still find its magnetism as enduring as the rock, which is millions of years old. At the end of a day out, we always want to go back.

Recently, we ended up on a route where I had one of my scariest falls soon after I had started climbing in 1994. We climbed the traverse – which means you move sideways, rather than up – as an easier option this time round, after I had persuaded Marianne and a friend of ours, Mark Seuring, to break up the hard routes with gentler pitches. They are both exceptional, sponsored climbers and were happy to climb within my ability.

Despite fearing the traverse, I found enough holds to feel solid, and with Marianne leading stylishly – the leader takes all the risk – we did ascents that were demanding and spectacular.

But not all climbing here is exposed and difficult. The mountain has some beautiful climbs that are

OPPOSITE: *Marianne climbing on Table Mountain*
LEFT: *Sailing races take place on Wednesday nights in Table Bay*
ABOVE: *Cycling from Simonstown to Cape Point*

also easy enough for a beginner to enjoy, like the classics Staircase and Jacob's Ladder on cliffs close to the cable car. I have taken friends who have never climbed before up these routes, which are described in Tony Lourens's climbing guide *Table Mountain Classics*.

BY FOOT

For people who prefer a swift ascent, the aerial cableway is a good option. Table Mountain has a range of hikes of varying lengths from the marked paths at the top to a few hours of hiking and full-day outings.

I was a teenager the first time I hiked up the mountain with a friend. I loved that first hike up Skeleton Gorge to the top (marked by Maclear's Beacon), and my legs were shaking by the time we got down to the cableway station, via a more exposed route known as India Venster. Now we often go up or down this route, as it provides the closest access to the climbing.

The hikes on Table Mountain are safe, as long as you follow the guidelines for hiking (see 'Hiking tips'). Weather conditions on the mountain can change swiftly if the tablecloth comes down, shrouding it in cold clouds, or if the wind picks up.

One of the world's best base jumpers, Jeb Corliss, did successful flights off the top in a wingsuit (a jumpsuit with wings to give the body extra lift) in 2012, following which he said: 'My programme is overcoming fear and this place scared me. Now, all of a sudden, I'm not scared of Table Mountain any more. It's become my playground.' But then, Corliss flew low between the boulders with inches to spare. He crashed at about 160 km/h, possibly from a gust, surviving with multiple injuries. 'I took the risk and paid the price for pushing way too hard,' he said of his accident. But, like most visitors, he intends to go back.

POPULAR HIKES
Platteklip Gorge attracts many hikers. The path starts about 1.5 kilometres past the lower cableway station. You walk up to a contour path and follow signs to the top. Table Mountain Walks (www.tablemountainwalks. co.za) estimates the hike takes three to four hours.

From the top, India Venster has a sign that reads 'This is not an easy way down', and the same applies to walking up this route, too. If you are walking-fit and willing to scramble – that is, do some steep or long step-ups, when you'll need to use your arms too – you'll enjoy it. The route starts about 50 metres to the right of the lower cableway station. It takes between two and four hours one way.

Skeleton Gorge starts from Kirstenbosch Gardens in Newlands. It's about five hours one way.

HIKING TIPS
Wear comfortable boots or shoes; take sunscreen, water, snacks, warm clothes and a phone. Go in clear weather and in a group, unless you know the path and feel confident alone. Table Mountain Watch monitors personal security on the mountain.

COME ALONG FOR THE RIDE
If you cycle from Simonstown to

Cape Point you might spot whales and penguins or run into Chacma baboons. These are among the only baboon troops in Africa known to eat seafood and we saw them grooming each other in the sun during an early-morning ride.

My favourite route starts with coffee and croissants at Olympia Cafe Deli, Kalk Bay, and traces the coastline, with the sea on one side and the mountains looming on the other (roughly a 40-kilometre return trip). But to reduce the distance, you can take the train to Simonstown and start from the station.

At dawn, on a windless morning before the traffic builds up, this ride must be one of the best in the world. The Cape Argus Cycle Tour includes this stretch – past Fish Hoek, Glencairn, Simonstown and Miller's Point. The Argus is now the biggest

timed cycling race in the world. In 2012, about 30 000 cyclists hit the road; when I first did it in the 1980s, there were a few thousand – without helmets.

CHAPMAN'S PEAK CYCLE
Chapman's Peak Drive is also along the Cape Argus Cycle Tour. Every time I'm in Cape Town, I cycle along this winding road and back, which runs from Hout Bay to Noordhoek and back (about 22 kilometres return).

Occasionally I lope behind my marathon-runner sister to the top or run on the mountain trail. The views across the bay to Sentinel Peak and over Noordhoek's 8-kilometre white beach are mesmerising.

One morning I cycled over Chapman's Peak to meet friends in Noordhoek, who picked me up (and my bike) en route to one of South

Africa's premier sport-climbing crags at Silvermine.

STERLING SILVER

Silvermine is a sport-climbing paradise with more than 80 long bolted climbs, from beginner grade to technically tough. To reach the climbs, you hike through fynbos, towards a mountain ridge. From the crest, you step over fallen trees and take a winding path down to the base of the cliffs. Five-star routes with names like Sterling Silver stand out but the crags also have four-star classics like Cool Hand Luke and Vlad the Impaler.

From the base of the climbs, you look out to sea with the forest below. My son enjoys playing among the rocks and caves. The burnt-orange sandstone is eroded into curious shapes, which provide solid holds for ascent, and the texture is great for balancing unless it rains and turns to glass.

The Silvermine Nature Reserve falls roughly in the middle of the Table Mountain National Park, near the Constantiaberg Mountain ridge, perched high up between Tokai and Hout Bay. The reserve has popular marked mountain-bike trails. For an easy walk, follow a boardwalk path around the reservoir; on the other side (10–15 minutes' walk) are picnic and braai spots.

PIGS AND PENGUINS

Imhoff Farm, near Noordhoek, is another family-friendly spot, where children can play with farm animals and watch horses in their paddocks. An organic deli, bakery, restaurant and bookstore are among the attractions.

Across the mountain in Simonstown, Boulders Beach (part of Table Mountain National Park) is the perfect beach for children. African Jackass penguins perch on rocks and swim in the calm turquoise sea with you. Big boulders shelter the swimming bay from most Cape winds, and scrambling up and under these rocks is fun for kids and adults.

When you need refuelling, Boulder's Beach Restaurant and Lodge has an outstanding chef and menu. The restaurant is decorated with wood sculptures by Jacques Dhont and has a deck with a sea view.

NOORDHOEK HORSE RIDING

Galloping your horse along Noordhoek Beach is forbidden, but you are allowed to canter, and the horses at Imhoff Equestrian Centre are both agile and fast.

My horse, Chelsea, decided to show off her speed on the 'racetrack', a stretch of packed sand away from the surf and people, and I got the exhilarating feeling of flying along with her. Marianne's horse, Rocket, did not live up to his name, however.

We set off together, riding in single file through a wetland with wading birds. On the beach we walked past the SS *Kakapo*, a steamer that ran aground in 1900.

The horses were calm when passing dog walkers, and trotted along smoothly until we headed for the hard sand. After the burst of speed, we returned to the stables at a chilled pace, passing even more laid-back surfers.

IF YOU GO

When to go

Late summer, autumn and spring are great times to visit Cape Town, with February to April being peak season for foreign tourists. Cape Town has rain in winter but it also has sunny, crystal days. The Southeaster blows in summer and the Northwester in winter.

Contacts and rates

- Table Mountain Aerial Cableway: single trip per adult ▣; (reduced rate for children aged 4–17; save 10 per cent if you book online) Tel 021 424 8181; web www.tablemountain.net
- Abseil Africa has a commercial drop into space at 1 000 metres above sea level; per person ▣. Their station and ropes are set up near the cableway station. Tel 021 424 4760; web www.abseilafrica.co.za
- For a climbing guide, try High Adventure Africa. Tel Ross Suter 082 4375145; web www.highadventure.co.za. Also see www.mountain-guides.ning.com. To learn about climbing safely, visit www.mcsacapetown.co.za
- A recommended book on the walks and climbs is *Table Mountain Classics* by Tony Lourens (Blue Mountain Publishers)

- Silvermine Nature Reserve: open 7 am– 6 pm; entry fee ▣. Tel 021 780 9002 (gate) or 021 789 2457 (office); web www.tmnp.co.za; email tablemountain@sanparks.org
- Boulders Penguin Colony: open 8 am–6.30 pm; entry fee ▣. Tel 021 701 8692; web www.tmnp.co.za; email tablemountain@sanparks.org
- Boulders Beach Restaurant and Lodge, Tel 021 786 1758; web www.bouldersbeach.co.za; email boulders@iafrica.com; booking advised
- Imhoff Equestrian Centre: horse riding per person for two hours ▣. Tel 082 774 1191; web www.horseriding.co.za; email horseriding@iafrica.com; booking essential
- Imhoff Farm, Tel 021 783 4545; web www.imhofffarm.co.za; email info@imhofffarm.co.za

How to get there

Regular flights arrive at Cape Town International Airport from national, regional and international locations. The city is serviced by the N2 highway, which runs all the way down the east coast from Mozambique, and then changes direction in Cape Town and continues up the west coast to Namibia.

27

CHINTSA, GLENGARRIFF & MORGANS BAY:
BAYWATCH

Long empty beaches with shipwrecks, lagoons, coves and dune forests are common along the southern end of the Wild Coast in the Eastern Cape, also known as the Jikeleza Route. In search of the perfect wave, we stopped off at Nahoon Beach in East London, and Chintsa and Glengarriff. Easy living and jumping fish defined our summertime trip to Morgans Bay, near the Kei River mouth, with its pontoon ferry.

WHAT A RIP

I first stood on a longboard at Nahoon Beach in East London when my son was a toddler. I've been chasing waves ever since – though I live in Joburg. In the Eastern Cape I found my ideal break – nothing like the giants sought by hard-core surfers. This is a small wave that unfurls gently, left and right, onto Yellow Sands Beach, near Glengarriff.

I thought Muizenberg was the best beginners' break – that's why you will see hundreds of 'grommets' on the surf there in summer. This is Cape Town's longboarding haven and an easy place to find your feet. But Yellow Sands (about 20 kilometres east of East London) has a trump card: a zippy rip along the rocks that pulls you to the back with no need to paddle. The Yellow Sands Beach break scores two stars on wannasurf.com, while the point break scores four.

WILD OYSTERS ON WILD COAST

Wild oyster stocks are not yet threatened in South Africa and the recreational harvesting of oysters is permitted. Prana Lodge, in Chintsa East (42 kilometres east of East London), invited us to stay and go oyster diving, among other activities. Our guide was surfer Sean van den Berg, whose wife, Megan, manages the family-owned luxury lodge.

Harvesting oysters doesn't require diving. The beds are usually found in tidal river mouths or on shallow reefs and rocks just off the shore, which get exposed at low tide. We drove to a wide river mouth near Chintsa. Donning masks, we waded into the knee-deep water to look for oysters and helped Sean to pry them off the rocks with knives.

This was a novel experience but the mountain biking at low tide along Chintsa Bay, where the golden beach stretches for more than 20 kilometres, was even better (see cover photo).

We also went horse riding on feisty mounts, trotting past rock pools and cantering along the sand. If you've got time, arrange to bike or horse ride along the beach and stop for a picnic.

relaxing beach holiday, swimming and sandboarding down the dunes. (For other sandboarding locations, see page 192.)

South Africa's only sea-cliff climbing is found in Morgans Bay, mostly on cracks in the dolerite rock. The routes on the faces and pinnacles next to the ocean can get wet from the spray. The proximity of the sea adds another element to the climbing, and along the top of the cliffs there is an undulating hiking route with panoramic views.

FERRY AND PLANE

The Great Kei River mouth has one of only two pontoon ferries in South Africa for transporting cars. The mouth of the Kei is about three kilometres from Morgans Bay, and we went with the children to have a ride on the old-fashioned 'pont'.

We each handed over a five-rand coin for walk-on passengers ([•] per vehicle); the pont chugged slowly across the muddy river to the other side and back. The Kei River used to be a boundary of the former Transkei homeland under the apartheid government.

On the other (western) side of Morgans Bay, you can find a jet airliner in the middle of a field. Ex-politician Billy Nel collects old planes and trains, and opens them up for public viewings on occasion.

FLYING FISH AND CLIFF CLIMBING

The beach at Morgans Bay (62 kilometres east of East London) has dunes and a lagoon with glittery flying fish and crowned cranes. We went paddling in the shallowish Inchara Lagoon and had dozens of mullet leaping onto our sea kayaks. The water level and how far upriver you can paddle depend on the tides and rainfall.

A holiday village since the early 1900s, Morgans Bay feels like it still belongs in the last century, with a single shop on the hill, a family hotel overlooking the Indian Ocean and a campsite on the lagoon. We joined friends with their children in a large Cape Cod-style house and had a

ACCOMMODATION

In 1946 Ivan Warren-Smith opened the landmark Morgan Bay Hotel, which has been modernised by his grandson and his wife. Luxury facilities, like the

Milkwood Spa, are among the latest additions but the old-world charm of the hotel is still evident in the lounge and dining room. Guests can also eat meals and have high tea or cocktails on the deck. From the bar menu, the fish and chips was great. The hotel caters for children and has babysitting services.

Prana Lodge is set in coastal dune forest with access to the beach along a wooden walkway. It is unique among the casual Eastern Cape beach resorts, being a five-star establishment with seven grand, private suites. The overall design has an Asian influence but the suites are decorated with original South African works of art, Persian carpets and antiques, and the bathrooms have carpets. A private flowering garden with a plunge pool and patio enhance the ambience.

Crawford's Beach Lodge is a popular family establishment, with ocean views overlooking Chintsa Bay.

Glengarriff Lodge, set on a hill, has the wild beauty and holiday mood typical of Wild Coast resorts but is more modern than most. The lodge is 25 kilometres from East London. Stables have been converted into six double rooms (two with an inter-leading room) with ceiling fans and fine linen. The vast Gecko Lounge has a bar and opens onto a colonial-style verandah. The lodge is a hundred steps above the sheltered Glen Eden Bay and Bulugha River mouth. Glen Eden also has a three-star right point break. Breakfast is fresh and simple, while lunch and dinner, for instance a fish braai, are served on request.

IF YOU GO

When to go
The Eastern Cape coast from East London to the Kei mouth has a subtropical climate with abundant flowering plants, and gets humid in summer when it rains. Winters are mild.

Contacts and rates
- Rates are much cheaper out of season than the in-season rates quoted below.
- Morgan Bay Hotel: in December, rooms start at • per night. Tel 043 841 1062; web www.morgan-bay-hotel.co.za; email morganbay@telkomsa.net
- Inchara Lagoon: book camping and caravan sites through the Morgans Bay Hotel. In the holidays, sites cost • per site.
- Tanglewood Studio: this small, self-catering studio with a balcony in the forest in Morgans Bay is an affordable option. The studio is attached to a thatched-roof house, which is also available to rent; studio rates per person per night •, slightly more for a couple •; Tanglewood House per night •. Tel 043 841 1031 or 073 424 9071; web www.wildcoastholidays.com/morganbay
- Prana Lodge: per person in high season (November– April), rates start at • for B & B. Tel 043 704 5100; web www.pranalodge.co.za; email info@pranalodge.co.za
- Crawford's Beach Lodge is popular so book ahead. Rates start at • per person for full board. Tel 043 738 5000; web www.crawfordsbeachlodge.co.za; email chintsa@iafrica.com
- Glengarriff Lodge: rates for a double room •. Tel 043 734 3409; web www.glengarrifflodge.co.za; email jacquiglenbb@telkomsa.net

How to get there
You can fly to East London Airport and drive less than an hour north along the coast to Chintsa and Morgans Bay (turn off the N2 to Mthatha).

RICHTERSVELD: DESTINATION DESOLATION

28

NORTHERN CAPE

The lAi-lAis/Richtersveld Transfrontier Park, straddling the border between South Africa and Namibia, is a vast mountainous desert with the most exquisite plant life – and silence. Here, you're on your own. No cellphone signal, no electricity, no running water. There is one last petrol stop at the entrance to the park, where you have to sign an indemnity form.

OFF THE BEATEN TRACK

The distance along the N14 between Johannesburg and Sendelingsdrift, the entrance to the park, is 1 595 kilometres and it's a long, straight road. Past Upington, it gets briefly colourful with the Northern Cape vineyards next to the Orange River and towards the Augrabies Falls. We stopped in Kakamas to spend the night and walk around the falls in almost unbearable heat. A better plan would have been to stop for longer and paddle down the Orange through the deep canyons, then relax on the banks of the river.

We carried on to Port Nolloth, with its half-deserted, yet functioning, seaport, where we stopped for the night. The locals live a simple, embedded life with dreams of one day encountering the bigger world out there. It is also the last place to pick up any forgotten supplies at the well-stocked supermarket.

The road north leads to the forsaken town of Alexander Bay, a result of the 1925 diamond rush. It is no longer a high-security area and it's worth driving around just to appease your sense of curiosity and mystery. The last 90-kilometre stretch up to Sendelingsdrift is on good dirt road, and passes some of the old mining sites.

THE IAI-IAIS/RICHTERSVELD TRANSFRONTIER PARK

The driving in the park is slow but never too technical, provided you have some clearance. We headed for the De Hoop campsite via the Akkedis Pass, where driving required focus but was not beyond comfort. My only regret is that we didn't take more time along this stretch. This part of the park has a richness of flora that compels you to stop and observe.

There are eight campsites in the park with bush toilets and some have cold showers. But you need to take all your own drinking water – and take more than you think you need. De Hoop campsite is the most popular, as it's well placed on the banks of the Orange River with beaches and big shady trees. There are no crocodiles in the Orange, so when it gets really hot, the most pleasant place is a comfortable seat in the river.

Even though De Hoop has ample water to cool you down, my favourite campsite was Kokerboomkloof. The approach from the top of the mountain resembles more a kokerboom graveyard than a kloof. These hardy trees, also known as quiver trees, which thrive in sand and little water, are dying in some places yet flourishing in others. Scientists haven't been able to explain this phenomenon, although assumptions lean towards climate change. The campsite, however, has heaps of healthy trees among the big rock formations – a setting that is perfect to photograph in the right light. We had the place to ourselves; the silence and space are engraved on my memory.

We left the park after four nights and took the Helskloof Pass, which has high viewpoints over the ever-changing landscapes. Just 22 kilometres from the exit back to Sendelingsdrift, you will reach the pontoon that takes you across to Namibia. We spent our last night near the rim of the Fish River Canyon. The immensity of the canyon, the world's second-largest after the Grand Canyon, made me wonder about how, when I was eight, my parents took me on a four-day hike down and along the canyon. The only vivid memories I have of that time are camping with scorpions and waking

up one morning (we slept under the stars) with leopard spoor around our campsite.

There are a few items that made this remote destination more heavenly – like my hammock, a solar shower, the car fridge, a set of pétanque (a boules game), cotton sheets, down pillows and a few good books.

PLACES ALONG THE WAY

Vergelegen Guest House is a popular and easy stopover next to the main road just before you reach Kakamas. Their restaurant, with wines from the area, makes a perfect dinner after a long journey, and also offers a large breakfast buffet.

Bedrock Lodge, in Port Nolloth, is one of the original houses right on the seafront, with a farm-style appearance. We had a very comfortable night in the Grace Room followed by a home-cooked breakfast.

Canyon Lodge is 20 kilometres from the main viewpoint over the Fish River Canyon.

We stopped at the Canyon Roadhouse, 25 kilometres from the Fish River Canyon, for a cappuccino. The bar is in a warehouse filled with antique motor-workshop equipment and decorated with old posters and trinkets. They also have food on the menu and offer good accommodation – and a pool.

If you love quiver trees, make a detour to Keimoes to the Koms Quiver Tree Nursery, which has a large variety. They will supply you with a permit to own a quiver tree and deliver to your home. (For more about desert-based activities, see page 190.)

IF YOU GO

When to go
The Northern Cape has extreme temperatures, particularly in summer, when nights can stay above 40 °C. If you're going to do a 4x4 trip, choose another season. Even paddling on the Orange River can be uncomfortable mid-summer.

Contacts and rates
- Visit www.sanparks.co.za for details and information on planning a trip.
- Bedrock Lodge, Port Nolloth: double room ▣. Tel 027 851 8865; web www.bedrocklodge.co.za
- Canyon Lodge: per person ▣, but they also have a cheaper self-catering option. Web www.canyonlodge.com
- Canyon Roadhouse: Tel +264 06125 9372 or +264 08188 65788
- Koms Quiver Tree Nursery, Keimoes: contact Marina Bothma on 054 464 0195 or 072 374 9432
- Vergelegen Guest House: per person sharing ▣. Tel 054 431 0976; email vergelegen@electronet.co.za

How to get there
You can fly into Upington with SA Express – the only airline operating on this route, so tickets can be limited and expensive – or drive about eight hours from Joburg. By road, Upington to Augrabies Falls takes about an hour.

29

NORTHERN CAPE

ORANGE RIVER & GREEN KALAHARI:
THE GREEN MILES

The Orange River is khaki green. Camouflaged amid vineyards, the river slides through the so-called Green Kalahari in the Northern Cape. Floating down the Orange and sleeping on its sandy banks compel you to slow down and see the earth and stars from another angle. The Orange is not just another river. Like the Zambezi, it is one of southern Africa's great rivers, dividing countries and realities, the landlocked and the fluid.

The Zambezi marks the border between Zimbabwe and Zambia; the Orange delineates the border between South Africa and Namibia.

The river is known for its pounding waterfall at Augrabies Falls National Park, where cataracts drop 56 metres past granite walls. But for most of its course, the Orange twists like a languid snake through a valley of vineyards and the arid Richtersveld, allowing for leisurely rafting trips. And the Orange is one of the few rivers in South Africa where group camping on its banks overnight is allowed.

SLEEPING ON RIVERBANKS

There are rafting trips that launch from the South African and Namibian sides. Marianne and I have independently done four- to five-day trips with friends in the past. We remember those as being easy – rapids were scarce on that stretch of river. But it was so hot that it felt like we were paddling through air as thick as honey. At night we lay under dampened kikoys so we could cool down enough to sleep.

OPPOSITE: *Zonele Nzuza on the Orange River during the Green Kalahari Canoe Marathon near Upington*
ABOVE: *Walking around the Groot Aarpan on route to Ashkam*

On a half-day rafting trip recently, the temperatures were again above 40 °C, propelling us into a late-afternoon paddle.

KHAMKIRRI AND THREE-STAGE CANOE MARATHON

Gawie Niewoudt, a man with a big laugh, big shoulders and big faded river shorts (which I borrowed), runs the adventure company that organised our paddling outing. Unlike with other sections of the Orange, the Augrabies area has only two rafting operators. Gawie has lived in Augrabies since he was six. He has never left.

He set up the adventure company Khamkirri on the banks of the Orange near Kakamas, and it is a river institution. 'I bought this place from a friend of mine for lekker braais. I used to farm grapes,' says Gawie, who was once chairman of Grape SA. 'Then people wanted to paddle, and ride horses, and I started Khamkirri. My relatives are all from here, Askham, Garies. My grandfather, who was the last of 16 kids, was given four hectares here in a job-creation programme.'

Gawie is the organiser of a three-stage canoeing race, the Green Kalahari Canoe Marathon, a 99-kilometre route between Upington and Augrabies, which takes place at the end of March. (By road this is known as the Quiver Tree Food and Wine Route.) It is like an easier version of the Dusi Canoe Marathon.

Marianne and I observed the start and were then planning to raft in the dramatic gorge below the Augrabies Falls.

PADDLING PAST FISH EAGLES AND GEMSBOK

But the heat inside the gorge was more than 50 °C, so instead we rafted a nine-kilometre stretch from Paarden Island

ABOVE: *Local people show off hunting skills at the first Kalahari Desert Festival* OPPOSITE: *Wine tasting at the Orange River Cellars in Keimoes*

past vineyards over gentle rapids – the water was low in March so they were grade two at the most – to our take-out at the Khamkirri base camp. The paddling in our croc (two-person raft) was placid, with only Whisky Rapid requiring any steering, as we followed our competent and relaxed guide, Eric Olyn.

We passed fish eagles on the river twice and saw gemsbok drinking on the shore near Khamkirri. We paddled into the sunset with bats circling above our heads. A perfect end to the day.

Gawie said: 'The Orange is a gentle introduction to rivers and 90 per cent of the people who come here have never paddled.'

WINE TASTING AND MEAT

On our trip we got another taste of genteel living: tasting wines at Orange River Cellars. This winery, the second-biggest wine cooperative in the world, produces an enormous volume of South Africa's wines – 10 to 20 times more than the entire Boland region. In the past few years, Orange River Cellars, under winemaker Rianco van Rooyen, has been winning awards for best value and classic whites.

Wine wasn't the only local speciality we tested: we also made a stop at the Kalahari Vleishuis butchery in Keimoes to stock up on biltong and dried sausage after tasting their lamb chops on the braai.

From Keimoes, we hit the road north to the Kalahari Desert proper, close to the Kgalagadi Transfrontier Park, which extends into Botswana and Namibia.

SAN DESERT FESTIVAL

We were invited to attend the inaugural Desert Festival hosted by the ‡Khomani San community on their reclaimed land outside Askham during the Human Rights Day long weekend.

This is a landscape of rolling red dunes and camelthorn trees, salt pans and open skies. From the top of a dune we could see forked lightning and thunder mounting in the distance.

This pilot festival – inspired by the Mali Desert Festival – was being celebrated at the //Uruke Bush Camp on Witdraai Farm, where there were a few tents and taps. The San community is developing this as a remote campsite for visitors to get away from the 21st-century world.

We found ourselves in a sudden rainstorm but, undeterred, our guides demonstrated how to use a bow and arrow made of wood and skin. A hunter who was younger than our official instructor struck the target (a plastic bottle) dead centre.

We also listened to marimba bands and watched the dance performance Seep in the main tent before musicians, including Pops Mohamed, performed.

Back in our rooms in the Molopo Lodge, popular among overland travellers, we could hear the songs from far away.

The Kalahari in the Northern Cape is a remote place. But, like the Orange River, if you've got the time to experience a different reality, it's worth it.

IF YOU GO

When to go
The Northern Cape has extreme temperatures, particularly in summer, when nights can stay above 40 °C. If you're going to do a 4x4 trip, choose another season. Even paddling on the Orange River can be uncomfortable mid-summer.

Contacts and rates
- For more information about the area, visit www.experiencenortherncape.com
- Khamkirri Adventure Destination and Game Farm offers rafting, kayaking, multi-day river trips, fly fishing, mountain biking and game drives. Half-day rafting trips ●; a four-day/three-night trip ●, all inclusive. Tel 082 790 1309 or 082 821 6649; web www.khamkirri.co.za; email info@khamkirri.co.za

How to get there
You can fly into Upington with SA Express – the only airline operating on this route, so tickets can be limited and expensive – or drive about eight hours from Joburg. By road, Upington to Augrabies Falls takes about an hour. Khamkirri Adventure Destination is near to Augrabies.

30 SPITZKOPPE & SWAKOPMUND:
GRANITE SERENITY

On the edge of the Namib Desert is a remote camp hidden away among granite formations, the most impressive of which is the towering Great Spitzkoppe. This is a true wilderness, a place to dream, beyond cellphone signal and the demands of modern life.

Marianne and I were alone in the vast space of the Gaingu Conservancy when we went on a climbing and camping trip there. We saw nobody, and the only sounds that broke the silence at night were the wind, intermittent thunder and animal cries.

Those who visit Spitzkoppe and the Pontok Mountains fall under their spell, and, like us, they return. The sheer beauty of Spitzkoppe is a siren call to climbers, campers, overland travellers, photographers and stargazers.

When we went in March it was hot. In the autumn, particularly Easter, and during spring holidays, the campsite becomes more populated.

The Damara community, who live in a village on the outskirts, own and manage the rest camp. There are rangers at the park entrance, which has no fence; only the quiver trees keep watch.

NAMIBIA'S *INSELBERGS*

The stark landscape of the Great and Klein Spitzkoppe, and the other *inselbergs* (German for 'island mountains'), which erupt from the plains, was outlined by the setting sun when we reached the park late one afternoon.

The rest camp has marked sites with fireplaces, usually under overhanging rocks or trees. On a first visit, it's worth exploring the park before pitching camp. The prime sites have long-drop toilets built inside stone walls. We chose to sleep under the south-west wall, a steep face with a curving arch. On a previous trip, Marianne and a friend survived a freezing night on this wall – watched by campers below – after they had been forced to stop when darkness

fell. To get the optimum combination of maximum light and minimum heat, climbers hit the rocks before sunrise.

Spitzkoppe has many trails that are fun for children to explore, as well as scrambling routes up rough rock through arches into gullies and secret corners.

Unlike the true desert further south, Spitzkoppe isn't densely populated with scorpions, spiders and snakes. Some of the snakes are poisonous but it's more common to see dassies, ground squirrels and buck on its sandy paths. On a prior trip with friends, though, I spotted a puff adder sunning itself, to my son's delight. The snake didn't even stir when I threw a Frisbee towards it, although it slithered away later.

BUSHMAN'S PARADISE ROCK ART

Transfigured animals and elongated dancing figures are among the characters painted onto the back wall of an overhanging cave at Bushman's Paradise, in Spitzkoppe. This is to the east of the Pontok Mountains; when you enter the park, turn right immediately and follow a gravel road to the base of a large, sloping rock face. Where the face meets a wall on the right there is a chain at about waist height to help people hike up. The angle and ease of the walk reminded me of a path up Half Dome in the Yosemite Valley in California.

After you have walked over the top, you dip into an unexpectedly pretty valley with grass, trees and flowers, where you find a large overhanging cave. The art has been vandalised and damaged but Bushman's Paradise is still worth a visit.

HIGH IN THE DESERT

On our trip Marianne and I decided to climb a harder variation of the standard route on Great Spitzkoppe, nicknamed the Matterhorn of Africa.

If you are fit, unafraid of heights and have a sense of adventure, you could do this popular route with an experienced guide – even if you have never climbed.

The approach and pitches are long and exposed, so we started before dawn to avoid heat exposure. Nearly eight hours later, we reached the top, with its 360-degree views.

Thirsty on the descent, we were tempted by a shimmering pool below us but the water turned into a mirage of pebbles when we reached it. Luckily, we had only an hour's walk to the camp and the chance to swim in a genuine rock pool. After summer most of the rainwater disappears from the hollows carved out of the rock. We were lucky to have found a wide pool in which we could cool down and get water for washing.

Another swim, another braai, another thunderstorm. Star-struck again.

SWAKOPMUND: DUNE DESERT

The Dorob National Park, along the central Namibian coastline – about 90 minutes' drive from Spitzkoppe – has the world's only dune desert.

The unique plants and endemic creatures of these dunes survive on the fog that rolls in from the Atlantic Ocean nine mornings out of ten, and a wind that blows seeds into the corners of the dunes. Beetles and silverfish eat the seeds; the bugs get hunted by geckos, lizards and chameleons, which, in turn, get devoured by snakes, jackals and falcons. Our guide, Christopher Nel, followed the faint tracks of the dune creatures and found all of the 'little five': the Namaqua chameleon (*Chamaeleo namaquensis*); the dancing white lady spider (*Carparachne aureoflava*); the Namib dune gecko (*Pachydactylus rangei*); the Fitzsimon's burrowing skink (*Typhlacontias brevipes*); and Peringuey's adder (*Bitis peringueyi*) – despite their masterful camouflage.

Chris, a surfer with a safari hat, where he once had blond dreads, is passionate about sharing his knowledge and promoting conservation through his company, Living Desert Adventures, so make sure to contact him if you come here. He can find desert secrets where the uninitiated, like us, see nothing. When he pointed out a patch of marbled sand under a small bush, for example, we looked in vain for life. Nel had spotted the eyes of a sidewinder snake from the sand in which it had burrowed. We could only see this small poisonous adder after Nel had blown away the sand. And the other sightings were just as astonishing.

Quad bikes and 4x4s have extensively damaged the coastal dunes, criss-crossing them with tracks, said Nel, showing us aerial photos of hundreds of tracks. The Dorob National Park now restricts vehicles to the off-road vehicle area (the dune belt) with a permit, and then only along certain roads and routes marked on the park's maps. We followed established paths in Nel's Land Rover, including descents where we had to hang on to the door handle and it felt like the vehicle was about to tip over (it never did).

STAR-STRUCK

If you want brilliant night skies, go to the desert. The Milky Way looks close enough to touch and we saw a shooting star that streamed towards us as if it would land at our feet – and that was with the naked eye, not a telescope.

Astronomer Dr Ansgar Gaedke and his wife, Lynette le Roux, run stargazing tours. Through the 10-inch telescope you can see extraordinary detail under these unpolluted skies. We were able to see the flares on Mars, the rings on Saturn, a globular cluster (Omega Centauri) and many more stellar beauties. Stargazing Adventures provides rolls and cooldrinks so you may want to take your own drinks for sundowners.

ATLANTIC VILLA

Atlantic Villa, a boutique guest house in Swakopmund, was sparklingly new when we stayed in its spacious, modern suites close to the beach. It has private balconies with ocean views.

THE JETTY AND VILLAGE CAFE

After camping at Spitzkoppe, any meal would have tasted great but the menu, presentation and quality of the food at the Jetty were truly exquisite. The Jetty also has a fabulous view, as it juts out over the ocean and the surf swirls below it.

For a backpackers' vibe and web access, go to the Village Cafe. This brightly decorated internet cafe has a relaxed, hippy feel and serves good coffee.

IF YOU GO

When to go

April and September are ideal times to visit Spitzkoppe, which gets very hot in summer and doesn't cool down as much as you'd expect at night. But in February or March you're more likely to find water in rock pools, which disappear as autumn approaches. Swakopmund has its own climate, as morning mist rolls off the ocean into the desert.

Contacts and rates

- For information about visiting Spitzkoppe, contact the Namibia Tourism Board. Tel 011 702 9602; 021 422 3298; or + 264 612 906 000. Rates per adult per night ◼; vehicle fee ◼
- Atlantic Villa in low season per person per night from ◼. Tel +264 064 463 511; web www.atlantic-villa.com; email bookings@atlantic-villa.com
- Stargazing Adventures: Tel +264 814 222 928 or +264 811 281 517; web www.stargazingadventure.com; email stargazing@iway.na
- Living Desert Adventures: Tel +264 644 050 70; web www.livingdesertnamibia.com; email nature@iafrica.com.na

How to get there

Daily flights are scheduled to Windhoek from both Johannesburg and Cape Town, and hiring a car from the airport costs roughly the same as in South Africa. But be warned that the airport is about 45 kilometres from Windhoek, so don't worry if you find yourself driving through semi-desert and can't find the capital! The drive from Windhoek to Spitzkoppe takes about four hours on a wide, open road.

SA Express and Air Namibia fly to Walvis Bay, which is half an hour's drive from Swakopmund along the coast.

31

MAKGADIKGADI PANS & CENTRAL KALAHARI:
SAFARI SO GOOD

BOTSWANA

The sun was low when Marianne, two friends, my son, Zade, and I crossed the 'great grey-green, greasy Limpopo River' into Botswana late in May. Our plan: to explore Botswana by road on a shoestring in 10 days. We made sure we were self-reliant and rented a fully equipped 4x4 with roof tents, water tanks, chairs and a table.

To cover nearly 3 000 kilometres, set up camp and cook most nights takes time and requires team effort so for this trip two friends, Lynn Morris, a top HIV scientist, and Jan Pirouz Poulsen, then a Danish diplomat, joined us.

But if you don't have the time or energy, and you do have the funds, you could fly to Maun, in the Okavango Delta, and travel to all our destinations in half the time.

KHAMA RHINO SANCTUARY

To reach this rhino sanctuary from Joburg was a solid day's drive in our double-cab diesel Nissan Hardbody: north-west past Mokopane, Limpopo, to the Martin's Drift border post and then into Botswana. At Palapye we turned west towards Serowe, watching out for cows and potholes in the dark. We tasted the national beer, St Louis Lager, at a roadside canteen. From Serowe, we headed north into the Khama Rhino Sanctuary, which is where we hit our first soft Kalahari sand.

The Khama Rhino Sanctuary has more than 30 black and white rhino, 30 species of mammals and 230 species of birds. The sanctuary lives up to its name and we saw nobody, only stars. The chalet has two beds in the living room and two more in the bedroom; it has lights and a hot-water shower.
In the morning, we had a breakfast in a clearing under a mokongwa tree, observed by yellow-billed hornbills.

MAKGADIKGADI SALT PANS

From Khama we headed north-west

to Kubu Island, a remote reserve of boulders and baobabs. We stopped to buy meat in Letlhakane, where fillet steak was then cheaper than chicken.

From Letlhakane, we drove north on a road that bisects the Sowa and Ntwetwe pans. Where the tar road ended and the gravel began, an information board welcomed us to Lekhubu (Kubu) Island.

Do all roads lead to Kubu Island? That's what we wondered after being compelled to choose a faint path – one of many – through the vast salt pans. We took only one wrong turn, but nevertheless the drive was slow: three hours to cover roughly 80 kilometres. But the moment Kubu Island appeared on the horizon, we were mesmerised

KUBU ISLAND

Granite boulders and baobabs rise like an apparition from the vast greyish pans, which used to be a mega-lake tens of thousands of years ago.

Kubu no longer has any water – you must bring your own – but enchanting trees and rocks offer refuge from the heat. The campsites are spaced far apart and we chose one with sprawling African star chestnut trees, providing shade and solid trunks on which to string up a slack line (tightrope). Our only visitor was the friendly manager, who sold us firewood from a wheelbarrow.

The Gaing-O Community Trust manages Kubu Island, which was declared a national monument in 1990 to preserve its Stone Age artefacts. Rock cairns, a ruined circular wall, cutting tools, remnants of pottery and a sacred cave with a shrine are among its historical attractions. We felt the mystery of this magnetic place while eating around the fire and falling asleep with stars dazzling us.

BLISS AND BAOBABS

'This is so beautiful,' were Zade's first words at sunrise when we went for a walk in the golden light. Energy levels dropped as the heat intensified. Time slowed and later, when the heat abated, we got onto the slack line.

Late in the afternoon, we hiked to the edge of the island, which has baobabs that look like dinosaurs and witches. Kubu has more than 60 baobabs in one square kilometre, some of which are 2 000 years old. We climbed trees, sloping rocks and chimneys, and walked onto the pan system, where we played boules. We wandered back to camp and had a relaxed evening.

Kubu is a popular destination for photographers because of its stark and awesome scenery.

KUBU ISLAND TO THE MATSWERE GATE

On another cloudless morning, we drove out of the Makgadikgadi Pans along its hazy tracks. When we reached the tar road, we turned right towards Rakops. The settlement was our last chance to stock up on water before we reached the Central Kalahari Game Reserve, 40 kilometres away.

We reached the park's Matswere Gate – its eastern entrance, which is decorated with the skulls of animals, including eland and giraffe – by mid-afternoon. At the Matswere recep-tion desk, visitors are given a list of information and regulations, including instructions to carry water. The recommended quota for the desert is 10–20 litres per person per day.

CAMPING WITH LIONS

From the gate, we drove to a campsite in Deception Valley – a secluded, shady clearing in the tawny bush. And you have no idea what is in that bush. A friend had a brown hyena come up and inspect his foot (and slink away) when he was camping here, and he also saw a honey badger. The Central Kalahari Game Reserve is unfenced, so animals move freely through the camps, which are scattered far apart across its 52 800 square kilometres. I woke up after midnight to hear lions roaring. In May, when we visited, much of the prey has migrated and the big cats are less visible.

SLOW SANDY SAFARI

A chart at the Matswere entrance shows when and where lion, cheetah, leopard and hyena were last spotted. We wanted to try to track down the Kalahari black-maned lion, made famous in the book *Cry of the Kalahari*, and the chart showed they had last been seen close to Sunday Pan. This was about 35 kilometres from our campsite, but the drive took us roughly half a day in the thick sand. The official speed limit is 40 km/h and the sand acts as a brake. In the Kalahari, other vehicles are spotted almost as infrequently as lions in winter. You need a 4x4 vehicle, spare fuel and water in case you get stuck.

SUNDOWNERS ON THE PLAINS

We heard lion but we never found them. We saw buck and other wildlife on the plains, and at the Sunday Pan waterhole. Among them were a startled-looking bat-eared fox scampering through the flowing grass, mongoose, black-backed jackal, gemsbok, kudu, giraffe and springbok. Above us were raptors like Bateleur eagles and falcons sweeping through the sky in the distance.

We drove on to Deception Pan for sundowners. The vastness of the plains has desolate beauty. After a glass of wine, we headed for our campsite. The site was more established than we had expected: there is a fireplace, a long-drop toilet like a throne inside a circular stone wall and another empty stone enclosure.

THE CRY OF THE KALAHARI

The foreigners to stay longest in the Central Kalahari – a land where San hunter-gatherers have roamed for hundreds of years – were American researchers Mark and Delia Owens, authors of *Cry of the Kalahari*. In 1974 the young couple wanted to study carnivores in an area where humans had not impacted on their habitat. They tell of how they woke up in their sleeping bags surrounded by a pride of nine lions in Deception Pan. In the book's conclusion, they write: 'We had lived through some difficult times in the desert, but the most difficult task of all was leaving Deception Valley.'

IF YOU GO

When to go

Winter is the best season to visit Botswana, which has extremely high temperatures and humidity in mid-summer. Besides the moderate heat in winter, the game viewing is better as the wildlife approach the waterholes, and the sandy roads are more navigable. But try to avoid school holidays if you want to get away from people.

Contacts and rates

- Khama Rhino Sanctuary: chalets per night ▪ and upwards; camping per adult per night ▪; park fees per day (for non-residents) ▪; vehicles per day ▪. Tel +267 463 0713 or +267 460 0204; fax +267 463 5808; web www.khamarhinosanctuary.org; email: krst@khamarhinosanctuary.org.bw
- Kubu Island is managed by the Gaing-O Community Trust. Camping per adult per night ▪. Tel/fax +267 297 9612; cellphone +267 754 946 69; web www.kubuisland.com; email kubu.island@botsnet.bw
- Central Kalahari Game Reserve: to book the designated campsites in Deception Valley (six camps) and Sunday Pan (three camps), contact Botswana's Department of Wildlife and National Parks. Tel +267 318 0774 or +267 397 1405; email DWNP@gov.bw. For more information, www.botswanatourism.co.bw
- To make reservations in the less travelled Passage (also known as Passarge) Valley, contact Bigfoot Safaris, Gaborone, tel +267 391 9954. The reserve also has a lodge in the north-eastern section for travellers wanting more comfort.

How to get there

You can fly into the delta frontier town of Maun – from here you have direct access to the wilderness of Moremi – and it is a few hours by 4x4 to Kubu Island and the Central Kalahari. From Joburg it takes about 12 hours (1 100 kilometres by road) to get to Maun via the Martin's Drift/Grobler's Bridge border post.

32

OKAVANGO DELTA: WAYS OF WATER

After travelling five dry, dusty days from Johannesburg to the Central Kalahari Game Reserve, the Okavango Delta, Botswana's most famous and popular natural attraction, was calling.

144

KALAHARI TO MAUN

We woke up on the sixth morning of our journey in the bush and sand of the Central Kalahari Game Reserve. By late afternoon, we were marvelling at one of the world's wet wonderlands: the Okavango Delta. These wilderness reserves are only about 100 kilometres apart, but the drive to Maun, the gateway to the Okavango, along sandy tracks parallel to a veterinary fence, took us hours.

DELTA FROM THE SKY

We reached Maun in time for a sunset flight over the delta. From the air, it looks like a gorgeous green, brown and blue mosaic, with palm trees and game adorning the floodplains and islands. If you imagine the delta fanned out like a palm leaf, the stalk originates in the northwest and Maun is situated on the south-east edge, at the tip of one of the central fronds. The aerial view gives you a unique perspective.

DELTA FROM THE WATER

The next morning, we were on the move again, this time by river. We trawled along the Thamalakane River to the Boro Channel and passed the Buffalo Fence, which marks the border of the reserve, and entered the protected wilderness of Moremi. It would have been faster to make use of our scenic flight the previous day and fly in. But the meandering trip through the channels was a chance to get to grips with the delta, despite the engine noise and sun. We stopped for a picnic lunch under a sausage tree along the way and by mid-afternoon we had reached our destination at Chief's Island.

DELTA FROM THE LAND

Chief's Island is the largest land mass in the delta. We landed at a shady beach, where we had hoped to set up camp. No fences divide humans and wildlife in Botswana; however, our guide, Gokgantshwang Eustice Tautona, was confident that my son would be safe, and the six of us set out on foot past the wild sage plants and high termite hills. There was elephant dung and spoor close to our cove.

At a point where the African mahogany, jackalberry and marula trees opened up onto a grassy plain, we came across a herd of grazing blue wildebeest, with impala and warthog nearby. Later, we could hear the snorting of hippos in the channel close to our camp.

SWIMMING WITH HIPPOS

Hippos rule the channels of the Okavango. From the shore, we could see pairs of ears sticking out of shallow water. We decided to swim in one of the pools, at a safe distance from any lurking hippos or crocodiles. Gokgantshwang cruised through the twisting tunnels to find a clear pool, where we dived in. We were all too aware, however, of the lurking dangers in the water. Five minutes after climbing back on the boat, we came round a bend into a channel teeming with hippo.

EAGLES, STORKS AND KIDS

Hippos, which help keep the channels free of vegetation, and therefore help keep them flowing, are plentiful in the floodplains and we saw more of them than any other big game in Moremi. We also spotted nearly two dozen bird species, including open-billed storks, saddle-billed storks, brown snake eagles, Bateleur eagles and countless African fish eagles. The cry of the fish eagle was our soundtrack as the sun went down and we got organised for the night. We made our own dinner, and our guide lit the campfire for the night, marking the end of our first 24 hours in the Okavango.

SLEEPLESS IN THE DELTA

Sleeping out – or, to be precise, hardly sleeping at all – on Chief's Island in the Moremi Game Reserve is an experience that stands out for Marianne and myself among the hundreds of nights we have camped across the continent. It's not every night you have hippos splashing near your tent or elephants strolling past. Our 'camping tents' protected us from the elements but they seemed flimsy against the giants whose territory we were in. Mine was pitched a safe distance from the water but Marianne's was on grass near a channel popular with hippos. At about 2 am, a loud cracking woke me and I could hear lions roaring in the distance.

I wondered how my friends were sleeping through the hippos grazing and snorting loudly. As it turned out, Marianne and Lynn were also wide awake. They'd got dressed in the dark and were expecting at any minute to have to bolt up the nearest tree. We greeted the first light with relief and

strong coffee, and watched a bull elephant metres away from my tent. Once the coast was clear, we motored off to Xaxaba Island.

XAXABA AND MOKORO TRIP

At Xaxaba Village, we found polers to take us on a *mokoro* trip. These traditional dugout canoes are gradually being replaced by fibreglass vessels to protect indigenous trees.

At a small market, children appeared from the patterned huts and we browsed through the local crafts, including miniature *mokoros*, before climbing aboard real ones. Enchanted by the sprites of the Okavango Delta, we floated through water lilies and dragonflies, losing any sense of time, tuning into the frog and bird calls, and watching elephant wade through the reeds. Too soon, we boarded our boat for a windswept and long trip back to Maun.

OLD BRIDGE BACKPACKERS

Back in Maun, we spent our second night at Old Bridge Backpackers, an oasis with lawns and giant fig trees on the banks of the Thamalakane River. We stayed in furnished safari tents with private verandahs, and en suite outdoor showers and toilets behind them. At the open-air bar, motorbikers chatted up blonde tourists to 70s hits such as 'Hotel California' and 'No Woman No Cry'. It was a classic backpacker scene, catering to travellers of all ages and budgets. In Maun we went out to the French Connection, a restaurant with an aviation theme across the road from the small international airport.

PLANET BAOBAB

The next day, we packed up our 4x4 for the last time and then, on our way out of Maun, lingered at the Kalahari Kofi Company Café, where laminated copies of the *Okavango Observer* from 1953 cover the tables. From there we drove south to Planet Baobab, near Gweta, on the edge of the Ntwetwe Pan.

The enormous baobabs are its main attraction, but Planet Baobab also has a massive swimming pool and a stylish Afro-baroque 'shebeen' with bar stools made of drums covered in cow hides. The rooms looked as enticing as the bar. We saw a spacious mud hut with an en suite bathroom, built along traditional Bakalanga lines and furnished with eclectic African art. We swam in the kidney-shaped pool, startled a stripy snake and had a satisfying lunch.

We wished we were staying at Planet Baobab but that would have made our next day too long, so we continued on to our final stop for the trip. Woodlands, near Francistown, is a well-maintained campsite with lawns on the banks of a river, small chalets and a country house, but Planet Baobab has more character. And, of course, baobabs – the last ones we saw before driving home to Joburg that night.

IF YOU GO

When to go
Winter is the best season to visit Botswana, which has extremely high temperatures and humidity in mid-summer. The Delta is filled with tourists in peak seasons.

Contacts and rates
- Mack Air (for flights over the Delta): for a 45-minute flight (five-seater) ▣ .
  Tel +267 686 0675; fax +267 686 0036; web www.mackair.co.bw;
  email reservations@mackair.co.bw
- Old Bridge Backpackers (to book Moremi Game Reserve): camping per night ▣ ; double en suite tents per night ▣ . Tel +267 686 2406; web www.maun-backpackers.com; Old Bridge Backpackers organises overnight self-catering inner-Delta boat safaris: one night per boat, including the driver and guide ▣
- Planet Baobab: per hut per night ▣ .
  Tel 021 855 0395; web www.planetbaobab.co
- Woodlands: per double room ▣ plus ▣ per extra person. Tel +267 244 0131; web www.woodlandscampingbots.com; email anneandmike@woodlandscampingbots.com

How to get there
There are regular scheduled flights to Maun from Cape Town and Johannesburg on legacy airlines. Boats and planes are the only way to get into the heart of the watery Moremi Game Reserve in the delta; trips can be arranged in the gateway town of Maun (for example, through Old Bridge Backpackers). Small planes do trips to the lodges and islands.

33 **ZAMBEZI RIVER & VIC FALLS:** WILD AND MIGHTY

ZIMBABWE

Marianne and I first rafted the Zambezi River in 2001 during a month-long road trip with a tent through five countries. We went on our own to cover stories on famine and HIV/Aids, avoiding potholes and armed soldiers. This was the trip when we really became friends. We took one day off to go whitewater rafting – we couldn't miss the chance – and had an exhilarating run down the mighty river.

In September 2005, I was back on the Zambezi training with the South African women's whitewater rafting team for the World Whitewater Rafting Championships in Ecuador that year. And in 2011, Marianne and I were back on the Zambezi – rafting below Victoria Falls and doing a canoe safari above them, and I bungee jumped over the river.

Despite rafting impressive rivers in South Africa, and from Nepal to the US, the Zambezi remains my favourite. Once again, our trip exceeded expectations. The stretch of river in the Batoka Gorge, below Victoria Falls, is powerful, deep, fast and fun – and safe. Most of the rapids are followed by calmer water, giving you a chance to catch your breath, whether you've paddled or swum through the foaming green waves.

READY, SET, GO

How often you end up in the drink depends on how experienced your river guide is, how well you work as a team and whether you want to experience the rush of being flung into the raging water.

Marianne and I rafted with Adventure Zone, which is based in Vic Falls on the Zimbabwean side of the river. Rafting is also offered from the Zambian side in Livingstone. Our day started with coffee and a safety briefing by our guide, Simon Moyo. At that point, all of the participants decided they wanted to paddle (you can choose to be active, or go along for the ride holding onto the flip line), and we organised ourselves into two teams. We climbed into the truck and headed to the gorge.

After a steep walk down to the river, we reached a beach. In this cove we practised paddling and crouching in the boat. What Simon said, we did: Simon says go down, we hit the deck.

ON THE RUN

On our trip, only rapids 11 to 23 were offered to commercial clients. From number 11, known as the White-faced Monster, we had an awesome run, sliding past a huge grade-five rapid – the highest rating is grade 6 – along the way. The other boat flipped on the Washing Machine and we picked up some of their swimmers.

By the time we had rafted the final rapid, they were in high spirits again and the Zambezi beers in the truck vanished in the post-rafting party at midday.

ROW, ROW, ROW YOUR CROC

You'd think that paddling the flatter water above the falls would be tame compared to the rafting, but it was thrilling too. Before we got onto the river – as the guests of Wild Frontiers – we signed indemnity forms again, the third set in 24 hours. The river is home to crocodiles, hippos and other dangerous wildlife.

For the canoe safari in the afternoon, we paddled in two-person inflatable rafts, known as crocs – not to be confused with the toothy variety sunning themselves on the banks of the Zambezi. Ironically, the surname of my guide, Mishack Ngwenya, means crocodile, his totem, he told me as we passed a juvenile one basking on an island.

UP CLOSE WITH HIPPO

One of the advantages of having guides is that they know where the hippos hang out, and Mishack would smack the water with a paddle to announce our arrival when we entered their territory. Our first sighting was one yawning ahead of us. When I saw its open jaws, I wondered again why Africa's big five are not the big six. Soon after, we saw a pod of at least 14 with only their ears and eyes barely visible and, not much later, we paddled towards a bull elephant near the water's edge.

As well as big game and monkeys, we saw plenty of antelope and birds, as well as baobabs, African mahogany and jackalberry trees, and a gorgeous African sunset to end our day.

REGAL RIDING

We had another two-hour safari experience in the Victoria Falls National Park, this time on the back an elephant. When we first got to shake trunks with the elephants at the Wallow at Wild Horizons Wildlife Sanctuary, they appeared to be calm.

After the safety talk, we moved to a loading ramp. Climbing up a ladder, we stepped off the platform into a saddle with seats and back rests. Our elephant handler sat at the front, I was in the middle and Marianne was at the back.

While we were waiting to move, the massive bull on which we were seated decided to push over a sapling, pitching us around slightly in the saddle. I realised then that we were at the bull's mercy – if he didn't want us on his back, we wouldn't be up there.

VIC FALLS PRIVATE GAME RESERVE

Once we were moving, the elephants loped along and riding through the bush on them was almost soporific. Sitting on elephants, you can get close to the wildlife in the bush, much like you can on horseback.

I'm sure that elephants must walk more quietly than Marianne and I did when we once went crashing through the bush on foot during a snare patrol in the Victoria Falls Private Game Reserve. On that patrol we saw not a single animal. But from the back of the elephants, we saw buck, birds and other animals, such as warthog.

We walked through mopane forest and grasslands alongside the Masuie River and crossed the river back to the Wallow sanctuary as the sun set.

ELEPHANT ETHICS

'The use of any animal for the pleasure of human beings will always be a contentious issue,' Wild Horizons acknowledges up-front in promoting its elephant-back safaris. The funds raised through elephant-back safaris help to support their rescue and conservation, the organisation says.

The wildlife team feel that the elephants under their management have adapted well to the sanctuary. Bulls have left the sanctuary and 'returned of their own free will; females have produced calves sired from wild bulls'; and adults have nurtured orphans.

VIC FALLS: WILD PLACES

The Chundu campsite, on the banks of the river in the Zambezi National Park, has no fences to keep out big game. Wild Frontiers set up a luxury bush camp for us with safari tents, together with a chef to cook our meals. You can also camp in the park as a private traveller. Traffic noises from the Zambian side of the river do reach the camp, but the sounds of hippos snorting and hyenas laughing are more immediate.

The comfortable Victoria Falls Safari Lodge is on a plateau and as well as hotel rooms it has self-catering chalets. The lodge's Buffalo Bar overlooks a waterhole, and the Boma, complete with drumming and a sangoma, is one of the town's favourite nightspots.

The Old Ursula Camp is a secluded getaway in the Victoria Falls Private Game Reserve. It has four thatched-roof chalets and giant trees overlooking the bush.

The Stanley and Livingstone Hotel looks like a colonial establishment, with animal trophies mounted on the wall and a faded charm. Old Ursula, down the road, is a satellite camp of the hotel.

The grand Victoria Falls Hotel, with its manicured garden overlooking the river, has an impressive high tea.

IF YOU GO

When to go
The climate in Zimbabwe is defined by the wet (November–April/May) and dry seasons (May–October). The end of the dry season is best for game viewing. If you want to run all 22 of the rapids commercially rafted on the Zambezi River, then aim for December to March and June to August, when the water is high. The low-water season is from about August to December.

Contacts and rates
- Adventure Zone: full-day whitewater rafting per person ▪. Low-water season is August–December, 19 rapids open; high-water season is December–March and June–August, 14 rapids open. Very high season, about March and June, rapids 15–24 open; web www.adventurezonevicfalls.com
- Full-day overnight canoe safari from ▪ per person. For details, visit www.wildfrontiers.com
- Wild Horizons elephant-back sunset safari ▪. Tel +263 134 457/426; web www.wildhorizons.co.za/elephants; email info@wildhorizons.co.zw
- Chundu campsite in the Zambezi National Park: overnight camping ▪. Tel 072 927 7529; web www.zimparks.org or www.wildfrontiers.com

- Victoria Falls Safari Lodge: per person per night ▪. Tel 021 683 7063; web www.victoria-falls-safari-lodge.com; email info@africaalbidatourism.com
- Old Ursula Camp: per person for a chalet from ▪; to book the whole camp ▪. Tel 011 658 0633; web www.oldursula.com
- Stanley and Livingstone Hotel: per person per night ▪. Tel 011 658 0633; web www.stanleyandlivingstone.com; email enquiries@raniresorts.com
- Bungee jump per person ▪. This 111-metre bungee with Shearwater Victoria Falls takes place off the Victoria Falls Bridge and I got to try it out soon after I had signed up and got weighed. The view is spectacular, even when you are hanging upside down. Tel +263 134 4471 or +263 773 461 716 (Reservations); web www.shearwatervictoriafalls.com; email reservations@shearwatervf.com

How to get there
You can fly to Vic Falls or Livingstone (in Zambia, across the bridge) in less than two hours from Joburg. By road, the trip from Joburg to Vic Falls takes about 12 hours (1 230 kilometres).

AFRISKI: TOP OF AFRICA

At 3 222 metres up in the Maluti Mountains, in Lesotho, AfriSki Ski and Mountain Resort is the continent's highest ski resort and the premier winter destination in southern Africa. This white wonderland doesn't have multiple graded runs or guaranteed layers of powder snow like overseas resorts, but nestled in an amphitheatre up the Moteng Pass, it has a magic of its own.

OLIVER SCHWANKHART

If you're lucky, you can float through powder snow like Marianne did on a snowboard one July weekend (I was on skis). The main slope, which has a one-kilometre piste, is visible from the top of the pass. Rising to its left is a freestyle snow park; and to the right is a beginners' slope where the ski school operates. The winter season is short, from early June until the end of August, but the snow is (mostly) real.

Though small by international ski-resort standards, AfriSki has lots of soul – and the festivity of a resort twice its size. The national skiing and snowboarding championships, bum-boarding races and ski-burning rituals are among its attractions.

The first time I visited with the Maluti Ski Club, there were no ski slopes, lifts or snow-making machines. We stopped at the side of the road and skied down the bowl, across grassy tufts if the snow wasn't deep enough, and walked back up. The transformation since 2004 has been remarkable. Now people who have never seen snow can learn to ski or snowboard; snow veterans wanting to flash their aerial skills can head for the park with its steep ramps and rails; and ice-climbers can test their axes on frozen waterfalls near the resort.

This mountain resort is now also open during the summer season for alpine hikes, Enduro motorbike trails, eco mountain-bike rides, pony trekking, fly fishing and athlete training. AfriSki truly is a playground for anyone, of any age.

'It's a pity one can't imagine what one can't compare to anything.

Genius is an African who dreams up snow,' wrote Russian novelist Vladimir Nabokov at the turn of the last century, unaware of Africa's snowy mountains.

LIPHOFUNG CAVE

On our first visit to AfriSki, we stopped along the way to explore the Liphofung (meaning Place of the Eland) Cave and cultural site, famous for its rock art. It also has a museum and cultural village. To reach the golden overhang, we walked across a tributary of the Hololo River above a deep cavern and waterfall. The first Basotho monarch, King Moshoeshoe the Great, used to stay in this large shelter, which has San rock paintings, when touring his realm.

From Liphofung, we wound our way past villages, cattle and goats up to the snow, through two passes, and finally reached our chalet at AfriSki.

ON THE SLOPES

I learnt the basics of skiing at the age of 32 in Salt Lake City (which hosted the 2002 Winter Olympics), where the powder snow makes for gentle falling. When I next skied, in Chamonix, in France, I discovered how hard snow can be. At AfriSki I've skied in freshly groomed powder snow and on a crisp main slope. We have experienced ideal conditions for skiing and frustrating weather – such as when gale-force winds mean that the ski lifts stop or don't run to the top.

AfriSki also has a drag lift and a rope lift on the beginners' slope and a travelator for children. Sliding or crashing down the bum-board alley on red plastic looks absurd but it is fun.

Roughly 70 per cent of visitors to AfriSki are learning to ski or snowboard. The resort has a ski and snowboard school with qualified instructors. And it has an intermediate slope with a button lift next to the main run (one kilometre with T-bar lifts) to cater to them.

AfriSki can accommodate up to 1 000 skiers a day. Most visitors are South Africans on day trips (about 400 per day during the weekends) or staying in the resort for a skiing holiday. During the working weeks, AfriSki has about 100 day visitors but during school holidays the numbers shoot up.

FROZEN WATERFALLS AND SANGOMAS

Training at high altitude in a place like AfriSki is the best way to prepare for mountain expeditions – for example, if you want to climb Kilimanjaro. Or if you just need a change of pace, you can hike through the snow to waterfalls glittering with icicles and frozen spray.

We walked a two-kilometre route from the resort to a half-frozen waterfall on the Motete River. This hike starts at the backpackers and runs south-east to the upper Motete River. It tracks the river downstream to the waterfall, which is about three metres high. The pool below it was partly covered in thick ice, frozen foam and a rainbow.

Adventure guide Martin Schultz and hiking and cultural guide Bongi Ramonotsi have mapped all the routes around AfriSki and lead guided walks. 'Most of the hikes you can do yourselves but we advise people to take a guide in winter,' Martin explained. 'The paths get iced and the weather changes quickly. I also do abseiling, depending on the snow pack and ice on the cliffs.'

Bongi loves showing tourists the rugged terrain. 'I also take foreign visitors to Motete village, where we visit the chief, the sangoma, a local shebeen and have a walk around,' he said.

MOUNTAIN FOOD

And for visitors simply wanting to admire the view, AfriSki has a restaurant and an après-ski cafe, both overlooking the slopes.

Built out of Austrian timber, the Sky restaurant is spacious and has a children's playroom. A pizza oven and wood stoves heat the interior, and photos of skiing in the Malutis since 1968 decorate the lounge. Cooking at high altitude is slower, so patrons need to wait longer than usual, and the service takes time if Sky is full.

The Gondola Cafe and Bar has faster food with a difference: it is fresh as well as filling, from breakfast wraps to chicken tikka. The red-velvet muffins and brownies are popular. And, naturally, it serves Glühwein any time of day.

After dinner on Wednesdays and Saturdays, you can catch a ski-burning ceremony in front of the Gondola Cafe, performed to invoke the snow gods. Holding lit torches, decorated with war paint and wearing Basotho hats, ski instructors hurtle down the slopes like flames in the dark. They ski across to a bonfire in the courtyard, where they chant invocations and place old, unwanted skis in the fire. After thawing out, instructors put on a show including a slapstick skit and a Jamaican calypso classic, the 'Big Bamboo'.

MOUNTAIN VIEWS

AfriSki offers packages in its chalets and lodge, and budget accommodation in the backpackers. The chalets look out over the amphitheatre and are minutes away from the slopes. They are comfortable and warmed by gas fireplaces, and well equipped for self-catering.

Down the pass, 16 kilometres from AfriSki, New Oxbow Lodge has en suite bedrooms.

Luxury accommodation is available at the five-star Maliba Mountain Lodge, about a two-hour drive from AfriSki.

About an hour further on, in Clarens and Fouriesburg, there is a range of accommodation close enough to base yourself for a day trip to AfriSki. (Find out more about skiing, snowboarding and ice climbing on page 198.)

IF YOU GO

When to go
The skiing and snowboarding season at AfriSki is open from June until the end of August. But AfriSki is also beautiful for hiking, abseiling and off-road motorbiking in summer.

Contacts and rates
- AfriSki caters for novices; instructors are available and equipment can be hired or bought. Full-day rental for adult skis, poles and snow boots ●; day rate for a snow pass, needed for the lifts ●; one-day adult beginner course ●; daycare per hour ●, per day ●; resort entry fee ●
- AfriSki gets full in season, so plan your trip well in advance. To book chalets, phone the central booking office on 0861 AFRISKI (0861 237 475) or email bookings@afriski.net. The resort offers packages from Thursday to Sunday/Sunday to Thursday, ranging from ● per person for three nights in a chalet to ● per person at the backpackers
- Hiking guides: per person for a half day ●; abseiling per person for a half day ●. Phone Martin Schultz on +266 597 95637; email martin@afriski.net
- Equipment is available for sale at the Gone Skiing

ski and snowboard shop in Johannesburg; contact 0861 SKI NOW (0861 754 669); www.goneskiing.com
- New Oxbow Lodge: B & B per couple ●. Tel 051 933 2247; web www.oxbow.co.za; email oxbowski@kingsley.co.za
- Mamohase Rural Stay: this B&B, 50 kilometres down the pass, has rooms in traditional rural homes; B & B and dinner per person ●. Tel Morabane on +266 580 45597; email info@mamohaseruralstay.com
- From South Africa, Clarens Xtreme runs trips to AfriSki. Tel 082 563 6242 or 058 256 1260; web www.clarensxtreme.co.za

How to get there
AfriSki is about four hours' drive from Joburg and Bloemfontein, and six from Durban. Access from Joburg is through the small Lesotho border post of Caledonspoort, and from there it takes about an hour (80 kilometres) to the resort up two mountain passes. These can get icy and snowy in winter and occasionally 4x4 traction is needed, but in other seasons a 4x4 is not critical (check website for road and skiing conditions). Don't forget your passport.

ACTIVITIES

OCEAN SPORTS: SEA KAYAKING, SURFING & SAILING

Mother Ocean embodies so many emotions that one can't give it a single definition. But one emotion probably that attracts all surfers, sailors and paddlers to the ocean's waters – something that expresses a constant longing in their eyes.

EQUIPMENT
All the equipment for the activities described below are provided by the various companies. For most of them, it is useful to have your own wetsuit or rash vest.

SEA KAYAKING
Sea kayaks are much more stable than whitewater kayaks or fibreglass K2 canoes. They are designed for long journeys in big, open water with a medium cruising speed and packing space. Kayaking is an easy way to take part in an ocean sport and get some exercise. I have seen schools of dolphins following paddlers behind the surf, which must be among the few things in life one should experience.

Great spots to sea kayak
Plettenberg Bay
Launch into the surf from Beacon Island Beach and paddle towards the Robberg Peninsula (see also page 94), where you can hear the seals barking. Closer to shore, the sea becomes shallow and clear blue. At the right

time of year, you may even see whales along the way.
Contact: www.oceanadventures.co.za;
Tel 044 533 5083

Hout Bay
From Hout Bay Harbour, on the Atlantic coast just south of Cape Town, you can sea kayak along the shore below Chapman's Peak or in the other direction past the Sentinel to Seal Island. Paddling among seals cavorting in the swell, with views of the rugged coastline, is a great way to start the weekend. Whales come into this bay in season (August to October, although one may see whales before and after) so you might spot them too.

SURFSKIING
This is a tricky sport. Designed for riding waves, surfskis are narrow, light and fast, which means they are unstable and can flip easily, but you cover a lot of distance quickly. With new technology, the boats have become more stable and this activity is not as far out of your reach as you may think. The feeling of riding the

PIC: GARETH WEIS

swell is fantastic and can get you hooked. It's not as technical and versatile as surfing, but you can get to ride loads of waves in the time surfers take to catch one.

Great spot for surfskiing
Fish Hoek

It is said that Fish Hoek, with its swell and wind direction, has the best downwind paddling in the world. Join a surfski clinic at the Fish Hoek Beach Sailing Club with Dawid and Nikki Mockes, who both have world champion titles.
Contact: www.surfskischool.com; Tel 021 782 4311

SURFING

Hundreds of years ago, an ancient Hawaiian tradition conceived the art of surfing. With basic boards, surfers relied on the *kahunas* (priests) to perform rituals and chants for the sea to provide them with surfable waves.

These days, beginner boards are more forgiving and lighter to handle, and we now have reliable wave/ weather forecasts, as opposed to *kahunas*.

Nevertheless, becoming a competent surfer is still one of the harder ocean-sport skills to master.
Contact: www.windguru.cz

Great spots for surfing
Ballito

There are no easy waves on the Durban North Coast. If you're comfortable on your board, the most forgiving surfing spot is at Salt Rock, where there is a beach and no rocks. The waves in summer are a lot calmer than in winter, apart from when cyclones come down from Mozambique in February.

This area is also known as the Dolphin Coast, and you're likely to get the chance to swim among these friendly mammals.

Muizenberg

Muizenberg, in the Cape's False Bay, has the best beach for beginner long-boarders, and on summer mornings the waves are packed. Beginners share the surf with talented youngsters and old-timers.

Gary's Surf Shop and Roxy's, both

across the road from the beach, stock everything you need to go out on your own, and can provide instructors. Dos Vacas shares the space with Gary's above it. The Knead Bakery and the Sinful Ice Cream Emporium are also worth a visit. (See also page 125.)

East London
Nahoon Point and Beach are famous for the consistency of the waves and 150 to 200 days a year of surfing, as well as being rated a world-class right-hand-break reef. If you have never surfed, it's worth finding solid instructors to get you started, to show you how to stand and to propel you into your first waves. (See also page 124.)
Contact: Gavin Wyness, veteran life guard and part-time surf instructor, on 083 348 6887

Chintsa/Yellow Sands
Chintsa has a long, sandy beach that is safe for beginners and the waves roll in smoothly. But at Yellow Sands nearby (20 kilometres east of Nahoon) is a long, rolling left and right break. The point break at Yellow Sands is highly noted for experienced surfers, but the beach break has its own advantage: a strong rip that takes you back to the break. This is a plus if you find paddling out difficult. Dolphins often play in the waves near surfers along the Eastern Cape coast. (See also page 124.)
Contact: Buccaneers Backpackers for surf instructors and board rental at www.cintsa.com; Tel 043 734 3012

Cape St Francis/Jeffreys Bay
J-Bay is world-famous for its supertubes, and the Billabong Pro

competition is held here in July. Surf-Jbay is a surfing school that gives lessons from beginners to advanced levels. Cape St Francis, 28 kilometres away, is less well known for surfing than J-Bay, but also has popular surfing spots like Seal Point and Bruce's Beauties, whose waves feature in the surfing movie *The Endless Summer*. The translucent turquoise water and rip current along the rocks make it a friendly beach break for beginners.
Contact: www.surfj-bay.co.za

SAILING
They say that when you come to love sea life, you're no longer fit to live on land. I'm somewhere in between: I like the idea of the sea, but can't hold my food down when I'm on a boat. So I've had to choose my moments, but I've experienced the exhilarating atmosphere of the winds and sails pushing the boat over the swell.

Great spots for sailing
Cape Town

Glamour and clamour collide on the yachts racing each other around Table Bay at twilight on Wednesday nights in the summer. If you are keen to join a race, you should go to the clubhouse on Cape Town's Foreshore (this means going through the harbour security gates, so call ahead to the Royal Cape Yacht Club) and volunteer to join a crew.
Contact: www.rcyc.co.za; Tel 021 421 1354

Plettenberg Bay

Towards the end of winter, the southern right and humpback whales make their way south. Very few outfits have a permit that allows you to approach whales from 50 metres, but sometimes the whales' own curiosity brings them closer to you, and you can get a very close-up view of them.

I've sailed out on a private Hobie Cat along Lookout Beach when a whale came right underneath our boat. (See also page 94.)
Contact: www.oceanadventures.co.za; Tel 044 533 5083

Hermanus Yacht Club

I sailed at Hermanus Yacht Club 30 years ago as a child and remember it as a fun place for the family to sail the Tempo, which is a similar class to the Fireball, with a trapeze and spinnaker. I remember it as a social and active sailing club, welcoming to members and visitors alike. But before you go, speak to the club or current members for details on what it is like now.
Contact: www.hyc.co.za; Tel 028 314 1420

SCUBA DIVING, SNORKELLING & SHARK DIVING

Scuba diving is a hypnotic experience – just floating along in a peaceful world devoid of the rush and noise that dominate life above the surface. Coral reefs, fish, rays, turtles, dolphins and sharks are among the wonders you may see when scuba diving.

Snorkelling has a similar charm but the swell and waves tend to demand more effort than when you dive deep under the sea. Shark cage diving isn't real diving, as you don't go deep or need a breathing apparatus. You are in a narrow, partly submerged cage and when sharks approach, you pull yourself below the surface and hold your breath to check them out at eye level.

SCUBA DIVING AND SNORKELLING

The equipment and boat rides necessitated by diving take some initial preparation. However, most divers willingly accept the time needed to prepare for a dive. At a minimum, qualified beginner scuba divers need their own mask, snorkel, fins and, ideally, a wetsuit and booties to be comfortable. Diving operations typically hire out the buoyancy compensator (like a life jacket) the breathing apparatus that attaches to the tank and the tank.

Snorkelling is simpler: you only need a mask, snorkel and fins. If you invest in nothing else, get a quality mask that doesn't leak or fog easily,

like a mid-range Scuba Pro mask. If you hire a mask and snorkel from a diving operator, test it in a pool first before you go into the sea.

There are many diving outfitters around the country. There is a comprehensive website with updated information about all the locations and contacts for the dive sites included here: www.divesouthafrica.com

Great spots for diving
East London: Wreck diving

I learnt to dive in East London, where the sea is often murky (many rivers flow into this coastline) and shore entries can be rough. But it was solid training and we had the chance to explore wrecks, another distinctive feature of the Eastern Cape Coast. I did one of my first dives with a buddy to a wreck just off Orient Beach.

Three Sisters is the best local reef, one kilometre off Bonza Bay, where there is cleaner water than you experience with most shore dives here. Wrecks of both the SS *King Cadwallon* and the *Lady Kennaway* are covered in marine life near the shore, and are great for

PIC: CALVIN BOTES

beginners. Winter is the best time of the year for diving on this coast.

Port Alfred: The Fountains

The Fountains is a popular dive site south-east of the Kowie River mouth, off Port Alfred. Apart from some pretty, soft corals, what I remember most – although this is nearly 20 years ago, so it may no longer be true – is that we often saw ragged-tooth sharks. These generally placid sharks tended to be bigger than us and would just cruise around.

Port Elizabeth

While Port Elizabeth is not known for scuba diving, it is an easy place to arrange a dive. There is even a reef within 100 metres of the old slipway in Algoa Bay, known as the Postman's Reef. The bay has several reefs and I did my qualifying dive at one of the reefs further out, I think it was the Wild Side reef.

Sodwana

Sodwana, in northern KwaZulu-Natal, has become the Mecca for scuba diving in South Africa with its two-, five-, seven- and nine-mile reefs. The corals and marine life are impressive but be prepared for crowds, particularly in the holiday season.

Thonga Beach

North of Sodwana are some pretty reefs with turtles, which can be reached from Thonga Beach Lodge (or arranged through them). I saw the biggest potato bass ever while diving here – the size of a small shark. The campsite at Thonga is in dune forest and a convenient base for diving, unless you want to stay at the fabulous luxury lodge.

Ponta do Ouro, Mozambique

Like Sodwana, Ponta do Ouro gets overrun by divers in the holiday season but out of season it's a relaxed place to have a beach holiday and dive. Even more appealing though for me was a dolphin-swimming experience – but this must be arranged through an ethical operator who follows the correct code of conduct and does not stress the dolphins. We went out to sea with Dolphin Encounters, who do research on dolphins along this coast.

You are not allowed to touch, crowd or follow dolphins (and only one boat is permitted per dolphin group) but when they choose to play among you, it's a special feeling. We also saw a school of sleeping dolphins below us. In deep water like this, and with snorkelling equipment, you must feel confident about your swimming and snorkelling to go out on such dives.

Tofo, Mozambique

Tofo, in Inhambane, is further north than Ponta do Ouro and the diving is even better. I had a fantastic dive there in clear, warm water with a wonderful array of marine life, including turtles and manta rays.

Archipelago, Mozambique

I snorkelled off Benguerra Island in the Bazaruto Archipelago, as I didn't have time to dive, and it was fun. From the surface, we could see luminous fish darting around below us and caught a glimpse of the coral life below.

Lake Malawi, Malawi

Lake Malawi offered a different kind of diving for me, as I'd never used scuba

equipment in fresh water. We had an enjoyable, relaxed time diving with an operator from Cape Maclear. I think I saw as much snorkelling in the lake off Cape Maclear as I did scuba diving from the boat further out.

SHARK DIVING

Great white shark diving, with its associated chumming of the ocean, is a controversial activity. If you are going to do this, choose an ethical operator who contributes funds to the protection of this magnificent species. (See also page 104.)

Great spots for shark diving
Gansbaai

The concentration of great white sharks at Gansbaai is remarkable – you may even see one of these giant predators breaching in the bay. The abundance of seals are like fast-food for the sharks, making Gansbaai a popular hang-out. More than a dozen cruised past the cage during our shark dive. (See also page 106.)
Contact: Shark Diving Unlimited;
Tel 028 384 2787; bookings 076 060 7187
web www.sharkdivingunlimited.com

Mossel Bay

White Shark Africa operates in Mossel Bay and they work with shark researchers like Ryan Johnson (see www.ryan-johnson.org). We saw plenty of sharks on this trip and one of the advantages of diving here is that the boat ride to Seal Island is short. (See also page 105.)
Contact: www.whitesharkafrica.com;
Tel 044 691 3796

FRESHWATER FUN: CANOEING, WATER SLIDES & CROC DIVING

We all find solace in water. Everyone wants to live on the coast, on the banks of lakes, by streams and rivers, and, ideally, on an island. Nothing makes small children happier than having the chance to splash through puddles.

WATER KIT

The companies hosting the activities generally supply basic equipment. These items are useful to have but not always necessary:

- Neoprene gloves
- Good set of goggles
- Wetsuits for cold water
- Neoprene booties or other water shoes
- Waterproof camera
- Sunglasses

CANOEING

Being on calm water in a canoe is a peaceful way to spend your day – especially with the easy-to-paddle canoes supplied by most resorts, which are stable and make canoeing accessible to all ages and abilities.

Great spots for canoeing

Nature's Valley

The Groot River Estuary runs through the lush Tsitsikamma Forest with its gigantic Outeniqua yellowwood trees and great wealth of bird life. This makes for an easy paddle, in two-man canoes, and there are opportunities to stop and explore the forest.

Canoes can be rented from the Nature's Valley Rest Camp, by the lagoon. (See also page 98.)
Contact: www.sanparks.co.za

Keurbooms

The Keurbooms River flows all the way from the Langkloof River to the sea, through unspoilt, unpopulated beauty higher upstream. Canoes can be hired at the entrance gate, just off the N2. There are a few beaches with braai facilities along the river, making it ideal for a day outing. The river can get crowded with motorboats during peak times so it is advisable to head out early. But the best way to experience the beauty the river has to offer is to do the Whiskey Creek overnight canoe trail, where you sleep in a remote, secluded log cabin seven kilometres upstream. (See also page 91.)
Contact: www.capenature.co.za; Tel 021 483 0190

Morgans Bay

The Morgans Bay Park has canoes for hire, and you can paddle up the Inchara Lagoon. There are plenty of fish in the water, which sometimes jump into your canoe. It is a very safe and calm place, which the whole family can enjoy. (See also page 124.)

Kosi Bay

Approaching the four-lake system of Kosi Bay takes you through thick indigenous forests made for fairy stories. The less frequented side of the bay has totally different, more tropical, vegetation. In our three-person canoe, we explored along the banks, spotting wildlife as we made our way along the lake. Fishermen in their narrow boats often appear from the reeds, going about their daily routines. The paddling here is very relaxed, enabling you to absorb the magic of this World Heritage Site. (See also page 54.)
Contact: www.kosibay.net; Tel 035 590 1233

Emmarentia Dam

The dam comes alive every day early morning and late afternoon with paddlers flocking to the dam for training. The Dabulamanzi Canoe Club is a great place to get into the sport on either K1 (single) or K2 (double) canoes. Swimmers also use the dam as a long-distance training venue and for water polo.
Contact: www.dabulamanzi.co.za; Tel 011 486 0979

Stand-up paddling is also taking off at Emmarentia. There are regular workshops on Saturday afternoons for anyone to try out till you're confident enough to train on your own during the week. (See also page 23.)
Contact: www.star-board.co.za; Tel 011 314 0795

TUBING

This is something most people probably did as kids – you would find an old tyre tube, blow it up, and throw it in the river or dam. Nowadays custom-designed tubes are streamlined to make travelling down rapids and rivers even more fun and comfortable. It takes zero skill – just a desire for fun.

Storms River

An adventurous river activity is to go tubing down the Storms River's Coca-Cola-coloured water. In winter, the water level is low and cold, and you often have to boulder hop in between pools – but it's still lots of fun. The summer months see more water and rapids to float down. Along the way there are some high boulders and cliffs that the more daring can jump from. (See also page 91.)
Contact: www.mild2wildadventures.com; Tel 042 281 1842

CROC DIVING

Similar to cage diving with sharks, you are safe in a metal cage while you are submerged under clear water to share the living space of these reptiles. Viewing them underwater and very close up is the latest novelty in wildlife encounters.

Oudtshoorn

Get up close and personal with giant Nile crocodiles at the Cango Wildlife Ranch, outside Oudtshoorn.
Contact: www.cango.co.za; Tel 044 272 5593

FUN IN THE WATER

If you don't like cold water, like me, jumping or sliding in a slightly daring way takes your mind off the cold. Most of the time, this is the only way I'll get in the water.

Meiringspoort

The road that leads through Meiringspoort, between Prince Albert and Oudtshoorn, crosses the Groot River 25 times. At one of these crossing is a long waterfall called the Skelm, which drops into a dark pool, said to be bottomless. The pool's cold water is a great revival for the weary traveller and the high cliffs are popular for jumping and diving off (if you're brave).

uShaka Marine World

uShaka Marine World is for all ages. Steep water slides, large tubes and a wave pool will keep kids busy for hours, while others will be mesmerised by the underwater world. As a non-diver, I could experience what it feels like three metres under water, walking along the ocean floor among rays, fish and coral, while breathing through a similar contraption to the original diving bell. You can also get into a cage that is lowered into the shark tank or watch the dolphins reveal their grace and intelligence. And there are numerous other novelties to get you closer to ocean life.
Contact: www.ushakamarineworld.co.za

Bela-Bela

I'm sure everyone who grew up in the old Transvaal went to Warmbaths at some point. Thirty years after my last visit, this place was pretty much how I remembered it – lots of pools (warm and cold, indoor and outdoor), slides, green lawns, ice cream and many kids. Some new activities have been added like the cable ski (similar to waterskiing but connected to a cable that goes around a large pool/dam). Kneeboarding and wakeboarding are also available.
Contact: www.foreverwarmbaths.co.ca; Tel 014 736 8500

Zambezi, Zimbabwe

In the big, flat, calm water of the Zambezi, above Victoria Falls, we paddled in two-man inflatable rafts and watched game on the banks. It's a thrill to paddle up to elephant drinking water, or spot a five-metre-long crocodile basking in the sun, feeling vulnerable, as we did, and part of the food chain. The guides in our boats understood the behaviour of animals, which gave us some peace of mind, but the many hippo ears that popped out of the water behind us felt a little nerve-wracking. Camping on the banks and once again watching the sun go down with a G & T settles you into the laid-back African life.
Contact: www.wildfrontiers.com; Tel 011 702 2035

Okavango Delta, Botswana

Motorboats can take you deep into the waters of the Okavango Delta. From there, a relaxing activity is to paddle in a *mokoro*, the traditional dugout canoe used by the local people to fish and for transport. The dugouts are surprisingly stable and you can watch game from the water.
Contact: www.maun-backpackers.com; Tel +267 686 2406

WHITEWATER RAFTING & KAYAKING

If the sound of big water makes you twitchy in a good way, and you need to feel alive, go whitewater rafting. The most important rule to remember is that the water is much more powerful than you and should never be underestimated.

In *Run the Rivers of Southern Africa* by Celliers Kruger, you'll find everything you need to get started and more about the sport and the rivers.

CATEGORIES OF RAFTING VESSELS

There are three types of vessels used for whitewater paddling. The most common is a six-person inflatable raft, popular for commercial trips. All passengers have a paddle; the guide at the stern steers through the rapids. These vessels can easily float over the big rapids that usually cause smaller boats to capsize.

Crocs are two-person inflatable rafts. Both people paddle while the person in the back steers. They require a bit more power to go over bigger rapids, but are stable and easy to manoeuvre.

Whitewater kayaks, also known as plastics, require more skill than crocs. You are on your own, tightly secured to the kayak with a splash cover that seals you to the boat. Kayaks are less stable than crocs, closer to the water and they cut through the waves.

If you know what you're doing, kayaking is a lot more fun and you're much closer to the action.

PERSONAL GEAR AND USEFUL TIPS

The technical gear for whitewater rafting is generally supplied by the various commercial operators that you book your rafting trip with. The following are items that I always advise to take along:

- **Sunscreen** – you burn a lot more quickly than you think on water. Reapply regularly.
- **Water** – choose a bottle that can be clipped to the boat somewhere so it's easy to rehydrate.
- **Shoes** – if you don't have kayaking booties, wear something that will stay on your feet if your boat flips.
- **Waterproof camera** – it's great to document these action activities and I always tie my waterproof camera to my life jacket where it's easily accessible to shoot.
- **Hat** – wear a cap that will fit under your helmet to keep the sun out of your eyes.
- **Top** – a long-sleeve top is the best

way to stop you from burning. If it's cold water, a wetsuit top is ideal. Thin windproof tops are advisable in case the wind picks up.

- **Gloves** – neoprene or cycling gloves provide relief against the wear and tear on your hands.
- **Dry bag** – for anything you don't want to get wet.

The Exploration Society of Southern Africa is a club of adventurers that often organises river trips and is open for anyone to join.
Contact: www.explorationsociety.org

Great whitewater spots
Always check with the rafting company that the river you're planning to paddle is in suitable condition (i.e. that there is enough water to make the experience worthwhile).

Vaal
The Vaal is one of the more accessible rivers. It is only one hour from Johannesburg and there is an abundance of river-rafting companies to choose from. You can select either a half-day or full-day adventure. The intensity of your adventure depends on the water level. The Vaal can get wild after heavy rain, but it is also uneventful when it is low. In summer, it is a very scenic river with lots of islands that break up the river into numerous side channels.
Contact: www.sunwa.co.za; Tel 011 431 2040 and www.x-factorevents.co.za; Tel 056 811 2344

Orange
The Orange is the longest river in South Africa, forming part of the border with Namibia. There are several rafting companies operating on different parts of the Orange. A multi-day paddle on the calm waters through the Richtersveld is essentially like floating through a desert (see also page 128). This part of the river is ideal for children and people with a low threshold for adrenalin keen to unwind in a remote destination.

Upriver from the Augrabies Falls is the Khamkirri River Camp (see page 133), where you will find easy rapids and relaxed paddling past beautiful scenery and some game. It can get extremely hot, so you tend to spend a lot of time in the water – luckily, there are no crocodiles in the Orange.
Contact: www.umkulu.co.za; Tel 021 853 7951 and www.bushwhacked.co.za; Tel 027 761 8953 and www.khamkirri.co.za; Tel 082 790 1309

Tugela
The Tugela is one of SA's most exciting rivers after heavy rains. Professional river guides check the river levels before they take commercial clients on, so it is likely that you will not experience terrifying conditions but enough big waves and churning whitewater to have fun. The Zingela bush camp arranges rafting in big six-person rafts, two-person crocs, or solo kayaking for those with a bit more skill (see also page 66). You can also book a kayaking training session and paddle the easier stretches of the river to gain confidence in kayaks.
Contact: www.zingelasafaris.co.za; Tel 036 354 7005/7250

Sabie

The Sabie River has some intimidating rapids, although they're easier to paddle than they look (all between grades 2 and 3). This is a good river for beginners as well as the more experienced rafter. The scenic lowveld landscape, with occasional wildlife, surrounds the river, and there are great lunch stops along the way.
Contact: www.indunaadventures.com; Tel 013 737 8308 or 082 463 2334

Olifants

The Olifants runs below the Drakensberg escarpment, close to Hoedspruit. It is a broad river with fun rapids – up to grade 3, sometimes grade 4 in high water – with pools below the rapids, where you can recover anything or anyone who has fallen out. There is an 11-kilometre half-day option, which includes six main rapids, or an overnight trip where you start on the Steelpoort River then join the Olifants, rafting through dry bushveld terrain with baobab trees.
Contact: www.extremelimpopo.com; Tel 071 480 9105 or 082 921 9543

Ash

The water of the Ash River is cold all year round, as it flows from the Trans-Caledon Tunnel from the Katse Dam in Lesotho. However, there is white water available for 12 months a year. There are a couple of grade 3 and 4 rapids to make for an exciting day out, but there are also enough gentle ones with long stretches of floating in between so you won't deplete your adrenalin resources. The constant flow of the water has carved out the banks to make it feel almost like a canal, with high walls in places. The Ash flows through farmland with good access by road to allow for either a half or full day of rafting. (See also page 78.)
Contact: www.clarensxtreme.co.za; Tel 058 256 1260 or 082 563 6241

Zambezi

The white water of the Zambezi River, below the falls, is big and wild. The high volume of water makes it safe, as there are few exposed rocks and more flow to move you through the rapids. It also makes it very exciting, with high, powerful drops. It is much more fun here to stay in the boat than to swim, so it's important to paddle as a team. The more power behind the boat, the better your chances of pushing through the rapids. Guides on this river are very experienced. I always recommend looking for the least gung-ho guide, who is less likely to flip his boat for fun. (See also page 148.)
Contact: www.wildhorizons.co.za; Tel +263 134 4571/4426

FISHING

I remember watching my cousins fish for hours while listening to cricket on the radio and couldn't imagine anything less exciting. Only recently did I try my hand at fishing and was surprised to find myself alert and absorbed in it.

The first bite, almost in disbelief, got me wanting more as I tried to predict where the fish could be. Before I knew it, hours had gone past and I had a great day.

GEAR

The basic equipment needed for fishing is fairly self-explanatory – rod, reel, line and flies. But when you get down to it, it's not that simple to select the right equipment. There is no such thing as an all-round outfit. Every fishing location – small streams, large rivers, salt water or dams – requires different gear. It's best to get expert advice from an established fishing shop to make sure you have the right equipment for your trip. I've also been told not to buy fly-fishing gear from someone who doesn't fly-fish. If you're using a guiding company, your gear should be provided or rented.

TIGER FISHING

There's a thrill to reeling in a tigerfish, trying to keep it and not let it swim off with your bait. With this fish, the regulations strictly stipulate catch and release, but we had enough time to check out their huge teeth before we let them go.

Great spots for tiger fishing
Zambezi

From a houseboat moored on the Chobe River, on the Namibian side, you can access the Upper Zambezi and Kasai rivers in Botswana with a small motorboat. Once anchored near the bank, you cast your lines and wait for a tug. After some brief instruction on our first fishing trip, we managed to catch five tigerfish with a rod, weighing around five pounds. I imagine this was due less to skill, and more to a good guide and a river full of hungry fish. Experienced fly fishermen cruise upstream on the Zambezi, sometimes for up to a month, in search of bigger, wilder fish. Contact: www.ngunivoyager.com; Tel 011 791 3101

FLY FISHING

Fly fishing is the most noble form of fishing and demands a high standard of fishing ethics from those who

pursue it. All fishermen I've met are fanatical about it. You either love it or hate it. But there must be something extraordinary about your passion if you often find yourself outsmarted by creatures so small.

In the Western Cape, the Cape Piscatorial Society issues permits to both members and the general public, subject to the regulations. The fly-fishing season here is from September to May.

Great fly-fishing spots
Western Cape

The crystal-clear streams of the Western Cape are known for their exceptional but technically demanding fishing. Most of the good spots are within an hour's drive of Cape Town. All fishing is strictly catch and release, and fly only. The non-indigenous trout are self-sustaining without need of stocking.

The rivers are divided into sections (beats) and booking an individual beat on a daily basis provides the angler with quality fishing uninterrupted by other anglers. Some, but not all, of the beats may be far from the road, requiring sometimes strenuous hiking and even some rock scrambling. At the more remote locations, you can turn fly fishing into an extreme sport if you choose to take the most difficult or distant terrain.

Tim Rolston provides specialist fly-fishing guidance and tuition (and advised me on writing the fishing section of this book).
Contact Inkwazi Flyfishing Safaris: www.inkwaziflyfishing.co.za; Tel 083 626 0467; email rolston@iafrica.com

Rhodes

The old-fashioned Eastern Cape town of Rhodes, which has a handful of permanent residents, has an abundance of trout fishing, with over 350 kilometres of fishable water. The high elevation and impulsive weather make the seasons unpredictable. Floods, drought and snow can occur in pretty much any month of the year but when you get the timing right, the fishing can be outstanding.

In the summer months, the

migration of yellowfish from the Kraai River up into its tributaries provides an additional aspect to the fishing; for the rest of the year, the focus is on the trout. Currently, trout fishing continues through the year without a closed season. Guidance is offered by Tony Kietzman (contactable via the Walkerbouts Inn in town) and Fred Steynberg.
Contact: 082 640 2930; email fred@linecasters. co.za. More information from www.wildtrout.co.za; permits are available from Walkerbouts Inn, Tel 045 974 9290

Cathcart

On the outskirts of the rustic town of Cathcart in the Eastern Cape, rugged terrain and grasslands unfold below the Elandsberg, evoking the Scottish Highlands on a smaller scale. The rivers of this area offer premier fly fishing and fishermen of all levels of experience head to Lowestoffe to fish the waters of the 17-kilometre Klipplaat River.

We visited Lowestoffe Country Lodge to try our luck. Despite an afternoon of casting into a well-stocked trout and bass dam under the guidance of farmer Neil Evens from Lowestoffe Country Lodge, we didn't get a single bite. He tried to improve our chances with wet flies, dry flies, sinking and floating lines, and different rods. No skill, no luck, no fish for us.

Skilled anglers will find trout and yellowfish in the river, but for a first-timer like me, it felt less intimidating to fish in one of the four stocked dams within walking distance of the Lowestoffe Country Lodge.
Contact: www.lowestoffecountrylodge.co.za; Tel 045 843 1716

MOUNTAIN BIKING & ROAD CYCLING

When I think about mountain biking, or any kind of cycling, I think dirt, sweat, burning quads ... and then the long downhill stretch as you freewheel into the breeze, free as a bird.

CYCLING ESSENTIALS:
- Gloves
- Cycling pants
- Helmet
- Hydration pack/water bottle
- Sunglasses

DON'T GO ON A RIDE WITHOUT:
- Water
- Food/snacks
- Bicycle pump, tools and spares
- Sunscreen
- Watch
- Cellphone
- Route plan of the area and trails

WHICH BIKE?
There are many different opinions and many options. The best is to start riding on whatever bike you have access to and progress from there. Some mountain bikes have full suspension, which gives a more comfortable ride, but these bikes are generally heavier and more expensive. Alternatively, there is the hard-tail type, which has only front suspension, is a bit more responsive and is a lighter ride in general. Mountain bikes are made for dirt road and

can handle rough terrain.

Road bikes don't have the suspension of mountain bikes. The frame and wheels are lighter and more aerodynamic, giving you greater speed to cover more distance, but the design limits you to tar roads. All the components can be adapted to suit the discipline you need the bike for.

For all types of bikes, there are many options to improve your ride. Cycling shops will help you choose the right sort of bike and the right fittings.

FIND OUT MORE
The biking magazines and their websites are a good source of information about gear, rides and advice:
www.ride.co.za
www.bicycling.co.za

Rides we can recommend
Giba Gorge
This mountain-bike park is used by some of the country's greatest mountain-bikers. It is just off the N3, in Hillcrest, outside Durban. The family-

friendly bike park seems to have something for everyone – over 30 kilometres of great rides of different grades, dirt jumps, a BMX track (and good-quality cappuccinos). The trail surfaces are smooth and a pleasure to ride. There is a small entrance fee, which also gives you access to a bike wash and hot showers. (See also page 60.)
Contact: www.gibagorge.co.za; Tel 031 769 1527

Clarens

This small village in the foothills of the Maluti Mountains currently has five mountain-bike routes through scenic landscape. The 12-kilometre village loop is a great introduction to the single track on this terrain before you move on to some of the longer routes. There's a mix of easy to more difficult rides; the most challenging is the 70-kilometre route that takes you over private farmland and climbs to 1 700 metres. The KTC shop in Clarens rents and sells bikes. (See also page 78.)
For GPS coordinates, maps and route descriptions, contact www.clarensxtreme.co.za; Tel 082 563 6242

Waterval Boven

This little railway town nestles in the rolling hills of Mpumalanga. The six cycling trails, mostly single track, take you over farmland, through forest and streams, and past red sandstone rock faces. Beginners can get hooked on the seven-kilometre forest loop, or the eight-kilometre rim ride. More advanced cyclists can link these trails with more technical and longer single tracks, and district roads. There is also a small jump track for kids to play on. (See also page 42.)

Maps and route descriptions are available from www.rocrope.com; Tel 013 257 0363 www.tranquilitas.com

Mankele

Not far from Nelspruit are some of the best single tracks through forests, grassland, rivers and mountains. The seven colour-coded routes are easy to follow and range from 1.5 to 55 kilometres. Routes can be combined for extra levels of effort and fun. There seems to be every option available, from beginners' trails to more hard-core technical rides. If you find cycling a drag, this is a place that would convert you. (See also page 48.)
Contact: www.mankele.co.za; Tel 078 801 0454

Karkloof

The Karkloof trails through forest follow bends and flowing lines with jumps along the way. The more risky sections also have a chicken-run option, which makes it a great place for riders of all ability levels. There is a trail fee payable at the country club, where all the routes start. (See also page 62.)
Contact: www.karkloofmtb.co.za; Tel 082 785 8282

Swartberg Pass

The pass links Oudtshoorn to the quaint Karoo town of Prince Albert. After cycling the gruelling pass, you feel less guilty about eating all that hearty Karoo food, as you have burnt off some calories. If you're not up to the challenge of cycling up this long pass, get a lift to the top and glide downhill into town. The total distance is 60 kilometres, of which 30 kilometres are good dirt road.

Baviaans Kloof

There is no better way to take in the unspoilt mountain wilderness of plants, animals, birds, trees and flowers than from your mountain bike. This World Heritage Site stretches for 210 kilometres between Willowmore and Patensie in the Eastern Cape's Kouga Mountains. A large stretch is on flat dirt road; the other half is a very steep and sometimes uneven mountain pass. There are lots of guest houses and campsites along the way to break your ride with the help of a support vehicle.

Cape Point

Catch a train to Simonstown with your bike and ride towards Cape Point. En route you might spot penguins, baboons and maybe even whales. It's a beautiful ride with a long uphill, but you are distracted by the surrounding views over the ocean. The return trip has a long freewheel at the end that will take you to some great coffee and breakfast spots in Kalk Bay.

Also on the Cape Peninsula, Chapman's Peak Drive, between Noordhoek and Hout Bay, is a shorter, sea-cliff ride (nine kilometres) and probably one of the best on the planet. Cyclists don't pay the normal toll. It is not recommended to cycle this route in bad weather, however, when the road is closed to motorists, owing to the unstable slopes.

Tokai Forest

This natural 'playground' on the slopes of Table Mountain is great for training and just 20 kilometres from Cape Town city centre. A dirt road leads up the hill to the mast (strenuous for the unfit), from where you start working down the single tracks back to the car park. The many forest roads make it easy to repeat sections of the single track, which can be challenging, or give you the option to join the single tracks without slogging to the top.

A fee is payable at the entrance before the car park. Take the Tokai offramp from the M3 towards Muizenberg. Follow Tokai Road to the ticket office and car park.

Harkerville

Between Plettenberg Bay and

Knysna are some of the best rides, single tracks and dirt roads, in the exceptional beauty of indigenous forest. Four colour-coded routes start from the Garden of Eden, on the N2. These routes range from fun family rides (11 kilometres) to more technical, back-breaking routes (22 kilometres). It is easy to link some of the rides to achieve greater distances. The Kranshoek picnic site is a great place to stop for a lunch break, with its magnificent coastal views. Permits must be obtained from the Garden of Eden at the start, where you can get route maps and information on other cycle routes in the area. (See also page 100.)
Bikes can be hired from Outeniqua Bike Hire, Tel 044 532 7644 or 083 252 7997; email bikesshop@mweb.co.za

Braamfontein Spruit
There are many mountain-bike routes around Johannesburg, but the Braamfontein Spruit single track has become an institution for mountain-bikers. One can start at any point and make your own loop, but the better sections cover Delta Park, Emmarentia Dam and the Albert's Farm area. The route is not marked, but the single track is obvious and there are many cyclists around to ask the way. (See also page 21.)

Van Gaalens
At the foot of the Magaliesberg mountains, 40 minutes from Johannesburg, is Van Gaalen Cheese Farm. Definitely a place you want to stop at and devour some of their cheese under a tree after a good ride. The trails, mostly single track, have been developed over surrounding private land, and are suitable for beginners and advanced-level mountain-bikers. The five routes vary from five kilometres, with chicken-run options, to a gruelling 120-kilometre ride for those in training. Route information can be found at the cheese shop, where a fee is also payable.
Contact: www.vangaalen.co.za; Tel 012 207 1289

Holla Trails
In the Ballito area, you will find at least eight routes, covering 340 kilometres among some working farms. This is a great spot for a whole family of cyclists – with the shortest ride at 13 kilometres to the longest at 82 kilometres. It is also a good place to start cycling, with easy single tracks and farm roads. More experienced riders will also find suitably challenging and exhilarating tracks. And at weekends you can fill up on a good farmer's breakfast.
Contact: www.hollatrails.co.za; Tel 082 899 3114

ROCK CLIMBING

Most adventure activities put you in extraordinary places that few get the opportunity to experience. They give you a feeling of being completely in touch with yourself and a sense of ultimate privacy.

Rock climbing has given me access to the most spectacular views and experiences all over the world – like slotting my fingers into a crack high up on a granite wall, surrounded by glaciers, while condors circle around, almost touching me with their wing tips.

Anyone can climb or abseil – these are safe and controlled activities as long as you use the correct gear, which has been tested to International Mountaineering and Climbing Federation (UIAA) standards.

There are many clubs you can join to get introduced to climbing:
- The Mountain Club of South Africa (MCSA) (www.mcsa.org.za)
- The South African Climbing Academy (www.saclimbingacademy.co.za)
- Roc 'n Rope Adventures (www.rocrope.com)

The Mountain Club Search and Rescue team is always on standby for emergencies anywhere in South Africa (Tel 074 125 1385 or 074 163 3952).

SPORT AND TRAD CLIMBING

There are two distinct climbing disciplines – sport climbing and traditional climbing (referred to as 'trad'). Most people start with sport climbing, which involves climbing on developed crags that have permanent bolts in the rock as protection. All you need to do is clip a quick draw to the bolt, followed by your rope, and continue like this to the top anchors.

Trad climbing, on the other hand, takes place on rocks that have no bolts. You need a set of camming devices and nuts to temporarily place in cracks for protection, but these are removed by the person following you. This style of climbing seems a lot more bold and dangerous, but it gives you greater freedom – you climb where you want to. Some believe it to be a purer form of climbing, as you remove everything you place in the rock and don't leave 'scars' behind.

CLIMBING GEAR

Climbing gear can be expensive if you buy it all in one go, but once you have it, it lasts a long time. The following items are the basic kit you will need to start with:

• Climbing shoes
• Harness
• Chalk bag
• Rope
• Quick draws
• Belay device with screw gate

The best places to buy gear are:
• Drifters (Sandton City, Tel 011 783 9200; Cape Quarter, Tel 021 418 4511)
• Mountain Mail Order (Cape Town; www.mountainmailorder.co.za, Tel 021 447 1319)

GRADING SYSTEM

All climbing routes are graded by their degree of difficulty. There are various grading systems in use around the world. In South Africa we use a system similar to the Australian one. The easiest grade is marked as a 10 and could resemble scrambling up an uneven, rocky staircase. From 15, which is a good beginner grade, it's like climbing up a ladder – not technical but you have to use some muscle. Moderate climbing grades up to 22 require some climbing technique, strength and endurance but are normally achievable with some training. Higher grades than 22 require a good sense of movement, and high levels of strength, focus and commitment.

Routes can either be single pitch or multi pitch. A single pitch means you can climb and abseil on one rope (normally 60 metres). Multi-pitch routes are higher and require climbing multiple rope lengths – this means you have to reach a point where you can make a secure stance, and from there continue with the next pitch. The term 'crag' refers to a length of rock with various climbs and usually has a name. 'Face' refers to the rock face on the specific route described.

Great climbing areas

The following are our favourite spots, but there are many climbing sites all over South Africa. Most route guides for climbing areas in South Africa can be downloaded from www.climbing. co.za, and the Mountain Club of South Africa's website is also a great resource: www.mcsa.org.za.

Waterval Boven

This old railway town in Mpumalanga is probably the most internationally known and visited climbing area in South Africa. Its prominent red sandstone faces offer a variety of vertical-face climbing as well as overhanging steep faces. On any given weekend, you'll find some of South Africa's top sport climbers at the crags.

There are many crags to choose from, with over 500 routes graded from very easy to very hard; there is easy climbing for children. There are safe camping facilities and chalets within walking distance. (See also page 42.)

Be sure to visit Roc 'n Rope Adventures in town for any tips or route guides on where to climb. Contact: www.rocrope.com; Tel 013 257 0363

Blouberg

The best-kept secret north of Polokwane, Blouberg still remains an intimidating mistress to climbers. The 400-metre wall requires experience in trad climbing. This is a wild place where people often get lost, stuck in the dark and run out of water. But to conquer the great mountain is a compulsion. (See also page 32.)

Harrismith surrounds
There are two well-established climbing areas on either side of the town, along the N3. (See also page 78.)

Eagle Mountain
Also known as Mount Everest, and just north of Harrismith in the Free State, Eagle Mountain is a small game reserve with grey sandstone cliffs. Most of the climbs (currently there are about 140 routes) are bolted sport climbs, most from easy to moderate grades. A number of these routes are good-quality multi-pitch routes. In between the bigger rock faces are big boulders with routes (28 crags in total) and they are accessible for kids.

Classic multi-pitch routes not to miss:
• Fight the Feeling (grade 21)
• Rhino on the City Hall Steps (grade 14)
• Power Pigeon (grade 21)
Contact: www. goeverest.co.za

Swinburne
This is south of Harrismith and has a wide range of bolted climbs, short as well as multi pitch. There are also hundreds of hard boulder problems among all the scattered boulders. Bouldering is a style of climbing where you don't need any climbing gear – you try a set of hard moves on a low boulder, usually 2 to 4 metres high. This is a good child-friendly climbing environment.

Don't miss the Starlings on Spearhead Boulder (grade 17) and Skinny Legs and All on the West End (grade 23).

Bronkhorstspruit
Less than an hour from Joburg, this is an easy day outing with a great range of grades, from easy to hard. Ideally, go early in the morning, as the sun hits the face after lunchtime. Great place for beginners and kids.
Classic climbs:
• The Fallen Boot (grade 15)
• If Women Were Gods (grade 20)
• Wasabi (grade 23)

Magaliesberg
The Magaliesberg mountain range has several kloofs with some fantastic climbing, mostly traditional, and beautiful rock pools. There are hundreds of single- and multi-pitch climbs of all grades. Most of the land

is privately owned but the MCSA has concessions to all of the climbing routes. If you are an MCSA member, you have free access; you can become a member or arrange a once-off permit from the MCSA.

Great kloofs to visit:
• Cedarberg
• Tonquani
• Boulder Kloof
• Groot Kloof
• Mhlabatini
(See also page 12.)

Kloof

Between Durban and Pietermaritzburg is the Kloof gorge system within the Krantzkloof Nature Reserve. The climbs are on eight different crags of all grades – most of them sport climbing, although there are some trad climbs too. Be warned: some areas require abseiling.

It is advisable to climb here in winter, as it can get very hot and humid in summer.

Monteseel

Not far from Kloof lies the Monteseel Valley, where you will find predominantly traditional climbing. There are over 300 routes with a range of grades.

Howick

There are a few good-quality routes on either side of the Howick Falls. An abseil into the climbs makes for some spectacular and exposed routes, with the constant thundering of the falls next to you. The classic climbs are Stagefright (grade 20) and Waiting in the Wings (grade 16). (See also page 62.)

Table Mountain

Everyone must climb on Table Mountain! Apart from the great location, the routes are superb traditional climbs. The options are endless, but the areas most frequently climbed are the Lower Buttress on the walk up from the cable car, African Ledge and Fountain Ledge, both high on the mountain, close to the upper cable-car station. The classic introductory climb to Table Mountain is Jacob's Ladder (grade 16) from Fountain Ledge.

Silvermine
In the Silvermine Reserve in the Table Mountain National Park there are a few sport crags with a good selection of climbs, most of them within an easy, child-friendly 15-minute walk from the car park.

Cederberg and Rocklands
Another jewel in the Cape, about three hours from Cape Town, these places rate among the best South Africa has to offer in all the climbing disciplines. Find out for yourself – take a climbing guidebook and climb as much as possible. (See also page 108.)

Montagu
About two hours east of Cape Town, in the semi-desert region of the Little Karoo, is the Cape's sport climbing equivalent of Waterval Boven. Hundreds of routes of all grades,

some along a river, make this a great destination for climbers of all levels, as well as a good family getaway.
For guiding and latest climbing information, contact www.montaguclimbing.com; Tel 082 696 4067

Oudtshoorn
A great limestone sport climbing area to be avoided in the heat of summer, although most of the crags get afternoon shade. It is known for its hard grades. There are a few easier routes but, ideally, you need to be experienced to climb here.

Spitzkoppe, Namibia
A giant free-standing dome of granite, nothing like anything else in southern Africa, Spitzkoppe is a unique climbing spot in its style of climbing as well as its desert location. There is a mix of sport and trad climbing (mostly trad and mostly multi-pitch). The general experience is an adventure with good climbing rather than just climbing per se. It is also a place to go with the family and kids, and there are some easier routes for non-climbers.

MARK SEURING

HIKING & CAVING

'Thousands of tired, nerve-shaken, over-civilized people are beginning to find out going to the mountains is going home; that wilderness is a necessity ...' – John Muir

HOW TO GET STARTED

Hiking is easy to get into because you can do it by yourself or with a group of people of all ages and abilities. Every town seems to have its own hiking club and outdoor enthusiast. The Mountain Club of South Africa provides comprehensive information and access to mountain hiking. Find your local section at www.mcsa.org.za.

The idea of caving makes some people cringe, but most commercial caves are lit and spacious with railings and walkways for easy access. Guides will tell you about narrow, tricky sections that you can choose to skip. The beautiful rock formations and cavities you get to experience make it worthwhile pushing your comfort limit a bit.

IN YOUR KIT BAG

Comfortable shoes will increase your love of hiking. A backpack with a good waist belt helps to absorb and spread the weight. A water bottle with a wide opening is handy for refilling at streams. Trekking poles are not just for old people – they lighten the workload on your legs, knees and back, and give you extra balance and stability. A pocketknife and torch should permanently be in your bag together with a small, compact first-aid kit. 'White gold' – also known as toilet paper – is a small but valuable commodity in the wilderness and should be buried, carefully burnt or discarded without leaving a trace.

Take a hike
Drakensberg

It takes just one visit to the Drakensberg to realise why it's a World Heritage Site. The Drakensberg is divided into three sections – northern, central and southern, all with an abundance of trails to explore. Although there are lots of gentle trails that take you through great locations, the real Drakensberg experience entails the long, gruelling uphill hikes to summits and caves set in a fantasy landscape. One can often see bearded vultures circling their territory. (See also page 70.)
Contact: www.drakensberg-tourism.com

Clarens

The Golden Gate Highlands National Park, which makes Clarens a great hiking destination, is not the only place to visit here. Motouleng Cave, which is big enough to house a traditional village of huts and is associated with sangomas and their rituals, is a fascinating, educational experience and a short walk from the car park. The Cannibal Hiking Trail, on a neighbouring farm, is a bit longer. There is a big overhanging cave to spend the night overlooking the classic mountain and rock shapes that define this area. (See also page 78.)
For guided tours or trails, contact www.clarensxtreme.co.za; Tel 082 563 6242

Lesotho

The Maluti Mountains border the Drakensberg, an area relatively untouched by tourism and with a wildness unlike anywhere in South Africa. Hiking trails follow the footpaths and herd tracks of the Basotho people. Sometimes you'll come across a friendly shepherd with his sheep, or wild horses roaming the uninhabited high plateaus.
Contact: www.afriski.net; Tel 086 123 747

Nature's Valley

Walk along the coast from Nature's Valley to Keurbooms, a 12-kilometre walk that takes about five hours. This includes long stretches of beach, some beautiful coastal forest and fynbos hills, two river crossings and ample resting spots with striking views to stop for lunch. (See also page 98.)
To book overnight accommodation in the Hikers' Cabin, contact www.hikerscabin.co.za; Tel 082 448 7953

Plettenberg Bay

The Robberg Peninsula is a spectacular nine-kilometre walk overlooking the bay. The full route can get dangerous and tricky during high tide. There are easier and shorter walks, however, that take you to the island. Try to book the Fountain Hut overnight, just past the island. It's an old renovated fisherman's hut with very basic but clean facilities in an ideal, romantic location. Your stay will be one of your most memorable evenings. (See also page 94.)
For bookings, contact www.capenature.co.za; Tel 021 483 0190

Graaff-Reinet

One doesn't usually think of mountains when you're in the Great Karoo, but the panoramic views from the top of the Valley of Desolation are superb. The short and easy 1.5-kilometre walk takes you past dolerite columns looking down over the Karoo plains and the town. There are three other hiking options that are between 5 and 14 kilometres in length, which start from the gate of the Camdeboo National Park (run by Sanparks), where you can find maps of the park.
Contact: www.sanparks.org

Gamkaskloof – Die Hel

The Gamkas Valley, known as The Hell, is hidden and secluded in the Swartberg mountains. People visit because of the interesting historical heritage of the area's inhabitants. The surrounding Cape Fold Belt Mountains are amazing and there are various hiking trails to follow in the valley. If you have time, it's worth driving to the end of the valley, on the Boplaas Farm, where the Ladder Trail leads to the top of the mountain. For many years, this trail was used to carry supplies down to the valley. From the top of the trail there is a fantastic view over the Gamkaskloof, where you see the many other hidden valleys radiating outwards – something the curious adventurer will enjoy exploring.
Contact: www.capenature.co.za; Tel 021 483 0190

Cederberg

The Cederberg is a rugged wilderness area with an abundance of hiking trails that wind through typical sandstone formations in fynbos terrain. The well-known Maltese Cross and Wolfberg Cracks are easy routes to start with, while overnight hikes to campsites or huts are still moderate but require a little more fitness. Most information on the area and permits can be obtained from www.capenature.co.za. (See also page 108.)

A unique long-distance adventure traversing the length of the Cape Fold Belt Mountains, from the Cederberg to the Outeniqua Mountains, is the newly established Rim of Africa Mountain Passage. This is South Africa's longest mountain

hiking route; it will immerse you in all the secret sites these mountains hold.
Contact: www.rimofafrica.co.za

Simonskloof

Situated between Montagu and Touwsriver, Simonskloof is truly remote, yet accessible. The stars and silence are almost palpable. Walking into the gorge through fynbos mountains and down rocky river beds is not hard or extreme – hiking here is manageable at all levels of fitness and bravery. However, it is a beautiful and peaceful place. A couple of short, quick abseils, which are well protected and not too exposed (and don't dominate the hike), lead you down to the water pools where you can mostly hop over rocks and avoid the cold water. Day or overnight trips are available with a guide; you can, however, explore without a guide.
Contact: www.simonskloof.com; Tel 023 614 1895

Hogsback

The numerous walks around Hogsback's forests and waterfalls have all the presence of a fantasy world. The information office in town has maps showing the routes for easy and short walks to long, multi-day hikes.

Magaliesberg

The Magaliesberg is my sanctuary from city life. These are among the oldest mountains in the world, with quartzite cliffs, crystal-clear streams, beautiful gorges and rock pools. They separate the highveld grasslands in the south from the bushveld savannah to the north. There are many walks

here, extending over an area of 120 kilometres, that allow you to explore the beauty of these protected mountains, and great care is given to keep the environment as clean and untouched as possible. Most of the land is private and permits must be obtained. (See also page 12.)
Contact: www.jhb.mcsa.org.za

Wild Coast

The Wild Coast is still one of my most enjoyable hiking areas. During my student years, I walked the different stretches along this coastline, generally over four to five days. The hiking starts from the Wild Coast Sun resort in the north to the Kei River mouth in the south, and covers a great variety of terrain, taking in beaches with cows, rural villages, unbelievable waterfalls, holiday spots, hotels from the 60s, shipwrecks and miles of beautiful coastline. (See also page 124.)

The ways in which you choose to explore this coast are also endless – slack packing, carrying your own stuff, cycling or even on horseback.
To help organise your trip, contact some of the established organisations in the area: www.drifters.co.za; Tel 011 888 1160 and www.wildcoast.co.za

Kruger National Park

It is pure exhilaration to walk through a big-five game reserve. In the process, you get to appreciate and learn more about the smaller animals, trees, insects and birds, and just take in the smell and feel of the veld. Two guides accompany you with rifles in case lions stalk you.
Contact: www.isibindiafrica.co.za; Tel 011 467 1886

Cango Caves

This is an underground walk that takes you through unbelievable dripstone caverns and chimneys of different shapes and sizes. The Standard Tour is a 1.2-kilometre round journey, accessible to all ages and abilities. The Adventure Tour (2.4 kilometres) is a bit more daring and daunting. The tour guides are resourceful in their knowledge on the history and composition of the caves.
Contact: www.cangocaves.co.za; Tel 044 272 7410

Sudwala Caves

The main cavern of these caves, the Amphitheatre, is 37 metres high and 70 metres in diameter. Lots of smaller caverns lead off this amphitheatre and there is a constant stream of fresh air from an unknown source. It is an easy surface to walk on, and the features of the chambers are illuminated. The Crystal Tour is an extension of the Standard Tour, but takes a few hours through dark, small passages with delicate formations.
Contact: www.sudwalacaves.com; Tel 079 205 1688

HORSE RIDING

It's the ancient relationship between horse and human that attracts me. When you're comfortable on horseback, you get to experience their grace and beauty, and sometimes understand their spirit and freedom.

FIRST-TIMERS

Hopefully, you'll have a good instructor to teach you the basics on your first ride. Here are a few tips, however, that have made it easier for me to feel relaxed on a horse:

- Talk to your horse before you mount it, and be calm. Horses can pick up if you are nervous, which will make them nervous too.
- Don't walk behind them without touching or talking to them, so they know you are there.
- Make it as comfortable as possible for your horse – use a mounting block to get on.
- Always maintain control over your horse. Don't let them eat while walking.
- Keep your heels down and use your legs for balance.
- Learn to trot before you start to canter.
- If your horse freaks out, don't scream. It will only make it worse.
- Be gentle with your horse.

Places to ride

Pakamisa, Pongola

With the very patient instruction of the owner of the Pakamisa Private Game Reserve, Isabella Stepski, I learnt to ride like an aristocrat. Her step-by-step discipline taught us how to saddle our horses, ride them and groom them afterwards before feeding them. Once she feels confident in your skills, you head out to watch game on horseback in the idyllic setting of the reserve. Horse riding allows you to get closer to wildlife and really feel part of the bush life. Isabella facilitates horse rides for riders of all levels.
Contact: www.pakamisa.co.za; Tel 034 413 3559

Kaapsehoop

Kaapsehoop, near Nelspruit, is best known for its 200 or so feral horses, which roam the forest in bachelor groups and some larger herds. Kaapsehoop Horse Trails treat their tame horses with love and freedom. There are many trails you can follow, but one of the more spectacular must be the ride that runs along the top of the escarpment. For the

more experienced riders, one can do overnight journeys in true western style through the old gold-digging sites and forests of the area. (See also page 38.)
Contact: www.horsebacktrails.co.za; Tel 082 774 5826

Noordhoek
The Imhoff Equestrian Centre in Noordhoek is a family-friendly spot, where children can play with farm animals and watch horses in their paddocks. The ride starts in single file through a wetland and then heads to Noordhoek Beach, where you can canter along the three-kilometre stretch of sand. The horses are calm when passing dog-walkers and surfers.
Contact: www.horseriding.co.za; Tel 082 774 1191

Chintsa
Buccaneers Backpackers runs a volunteer programme on their horse farm and rehabilitation centre, where volunteers assist in beach trails for clients. As a client, you ride across the four-kilometre stretch of unspoilt Chintsa Beach and return via the river and bush track, which leads you back to the backpackers. (See also page 124.)
Contact: www.cintsa.com; Tel 043 734 3012

Drakensberg
Riding like a cowboy in the Wild West is the experience of Khotso Horse Trails in Underberg. The well-trained, agile Basotho ponies inspire so much confidence as they climb the rocky donkey trail high up into the Maluti Mountains. Day rides are great, but the ultimate experience is to spend at least one night in the mountains.

At uShaka Horse Trails in Monk's Cowl Valley, the horses are placid, easy to ride, but not very active for more experienced riders. Higher up on the foothills of the Drakensberg, the view is great, making the ride more memorable.
Contact: www.khotsotrails.co.za; Tel 033 701 1502; www.monkscowl.com; Tel 036 468 1136 or 072 312 2659

Harrismith
Mount Everest Game Reserve has farm horses that don't go fast – an easy introduction to horse riding and ideal for kids. Guides walk the horses through the veld at a very easy pace – a perfect ride at sunset.
Contact: www.goeverest.co.za; Tel 079 886 3101

Oudtshoorn ostrich rides
The Cango Ostrich Farm, 14 kilometres outside Oudtshoorn, is family-friendly and offers 45-minute tours where you get to interact with these birds. Guides help you to sit on the ostrich correctly before they let it run free and you hold on for dear life, something easier said than done. The very quick ride is certainly a novelty activity you want to tick off your list. There is a weight limit of 75 kilograms to ride an ostrich. People of (almost) any weight can stand on the ostrich eggs for the ultimate strength test.
Contact: www.cangoostrich.co.za; Tel 044 272 4623

DESERT, DUNES & OFF-ROADING

I love going to places where there are miles and miles of deserted, uninhabited space. Maybe it's the minimalistic landscapes and monotones that attract me visually, while the sound of silence and the solitude feed my soul.

Do not disappear into the desert without: water; GPS; warm clothing; sunglasses; sunscreen; and a sun hat.

Places we recommend

OFF-ROADING
Richtersveld

The |Ai-|Ais/Richtersveld Transfrontier Park is a vast mountainous desert with the most exquisite plant life in a multi-earth-coloured landscape.

And silence. You're on your own – no cellphone signal, no electricity, no running water. There is one last petrol stop at the entrance to the park, where you have to sign indemnity. This is not a holiday you can rush – you need at least four nights in the park to do justice to the experience. The best time to go is during the cooler period between May and September. The busiest time, but also the most spectacular, is around September, when all the flowers bloom, covering the desert landscape in a blanket of contrasting bright colours. (See also page 128.)

You are completely self-sufficient and need to do your homework to plan a trip here.
Contact: www.sanparks.org

BOTSWANA
There are many things you will need to make a trip through Botswana. But the non-negotiables are water and a car that can drive through sand.

Kubu Island
I love the abundance of magical places on this continent. Kubu Island lies at the western end of the Makgadikgadi Pans, one of the largest saltpans in the world. So you can imagine the contrast between the miles and miles of flat earth and this sudden rocky outcrop with large baobab trees. Although it is great to explore the 'island' – with its old gravestones and unusual boulders and tree shapes – you really just want to absorb the landscape. The drive is slow and sandy, and you need all of your own supplies, including water and a hammock. (See also page 140.)
Contact: www.kubuisland.com; Tel +267 297 9612

Central Kalahari Game Reserve

The reserve is unfenced, so game moves freely through the camps, which are scattered far apart across its 52 800 square kilometres. In the Kalahari, other vehicles are seldom spotted. Deception Valley has a vast open pan where game roam in the rainy season. In winter, when there is less game, it is still a beautiful and nostalgic plain, perfect for sundowners. Sunday Pan, 35 kilometres down the road, where you can also camp, has a waterhole frequented by buck and sometimes predators. Distances between the many campsites in the Kalahari are great and the journeys time consuming. Booking and permits are essential. (See also page 140.)
Contact: www.botswanatourism.co.bw;
Tel +267 318 0774 or +267 397 1405

NAMIBIA
Fish River

Drive along the eastern rim of the Fish River Canyon, the second-largest in the world after the Grand Canyon. Start from Hobas, in the north, and follow the good dirt road with viewpoints along the rim of the canyon. There is a great variety of geological features in the canyon. The closest petrol station is about 20 kilometres away, at the Canyon Roadhouse. There is a tourist information centre in Hobas with maps and information on the area. (See also page 131.)
Contact: www.namibian.org

Spitzkoppe

The name 'Spitzkoppe' makes those who've been there nostalgic – a vast desert wilderness with huge granite domes towering over the flat land. Campsites are remote and scattered below the main 400-metre Spitzkoppe rock face. Walking around, you can find the hidden pool, Bushman paintings, an arch and plenty of great plants and boulders to scramble over. Experienced climbers have explored and established a variety of climbs of all grades and lengths. (See also page 136).
Contact: Namibian Tourism Board; Tel 011 702 9602 or +264 612 906 000

Swakopmund

The endemic creatures and plants of the Dorob National Park survive on the fog and seeds blowing in from the coast. Our passionate guide knew the behaviour of all of the little animals so well that he managed to track desert chameleons, sidewinder snakes, skinks, Namib dune geckos and dancing white lady spiders in one morning. Driving on the bigger red sand dunes on designated tracks, he pointed out the damage that vehicles make when they drive off the path. (See also page 136.)
Contact: www.livingdesertnamibia.com; Tel +264 644 05070

MOTORBIKING
Lesotho

Mountains and waterfalls dominate this 'kingdom in the sky', and the scenery is still wild and untouched. The rough terrain makes it a popular destination for off-road bikers looking for a challenge. Lesotho is the home of the Roof of Africa enduro challenge based in the Maseru region of Roma and Ramabanta. The rest of Lesotho offers endless opportunities for the bigger dual sports/touring bikes to go on epic road trips. High up in the Maluti Mountains, AfriSki has charted over 600 kilometres of both enduro and dual touring bike routes, including trips to the breathtaking Sani Pass and the various dams of the Lesotho Highlands Water Project. The high altitude makes for a good workout, with some spectacular landscape and viewpoints.
Contact: www.afriski.net; Tel 0861 AFRISKI (0861 237 4754) for GPS coordinates or a guide; www.tradingpost.co.za

SAND BOARDING
Alantis

The shifting sand dunes of Atlantis are hidden away north of Cape Town. The white slopes roll out into a blue horizon and are popular for desert film shoots. The boards are modified snowboards and the technique is similar to snowboarding, although a lot slower and less slippery. Falling is also much softer. You need a board with bindings, wax, sports shoes, hat, sunscreen and goggles or sunglasses – most of these will be provided. Once you get into sand boarding, it's great fun trying out different speeds on the steep dunes.
Contact: www.sandboardingcapetown.com; Tel 084 665 1314

BUSH: WALKING WITH GAME, ELEPHANT CONSERVATION & SNAKE HANDLING

Every country has a zoo, but not every country has big game that roam wild, or the chance for us to share the animals' environment with them.

We're lucky in South Africa to be at the heart of conservation that sometimes allows us to interact with the animals. From my many experiences with wild animals, I have learnt it is always important to respect the animals and remember that they're wild.

Places we recommend
Kruger National Park – Rhino Walking Safari
Walking in Kruger requires all your senses. Not just to be on the lookout for anything that may hunt you, but also to track some of the smaller insects and animals, and to observe their behaviour. I found myself much more absorbed watching a spider protect its nest, than a lion lying in the sun. You learn about the trees – their medicinal qualities and practical uses. Armed guides walk in front and behind you with a trained eye for any movement. Hiding behind an anthill, we watched two rhinos a short distance away without alarming them.
Contact: www.isibindi.co.za; Tel 011 467 1886

Zimbabwe – anti-poaching volunteer programme
At the Stanley and Livingstone Private Game Reserve, near Victoria Falls, anyone can become part of the campaign to save the rhino. The International Anti-Poaching Foundation provides a volunteer programme where you live the life of an anti-poaching ranger. Hands-on involvement with the patrolling operation, particularly during full moon, when poaching increases, can be more exhilarating than you think. During the day, you learn about the land and plants while looking for snares and mastering your tracking skills.

At camp, you look after yourself and perform the same duties as the professional rangers as part of the team. The daily activities change according to new challenges but in the end, the volunteer programme provides great support for this initiative.
Contact: www.iapf.org; Tel +263 774 659 474
There is a similar programme in South Africa near Hoedspruit; contact 071 309 0374

Mpumalanga – chimpanzee sanctuary
The Jane Goodall Institute provides rescue and care for orphaned chimps that have been misplaced from their natural habitat in Africa. Three groups of chimps in different camps have formed a new family hierarchy, as they would in the wild. Each chimp has its own personality and habits, and one can watch them from the viewing decks for hours.

The institute has also established a volunteer programme aimed at improving global understanding of chimpanzees.
Contact: www.janegoodall.co.za; Tel 079 777 1514

Botswana – Okavango Delta
A cheaper way of seeing the delta and Chief's Island is to hire a boat with a guide and camp out in the wild. My heartbeat has never been as high as when hippo and elephant walked within metres of my flimsy tent shelter. Their snorts and trumpeting take on a different meaning when you're practically lying at their feet. The roar of the lions further away in the bush seemed dull in comparison.

The waters of the delta are clear so one can also take turns to swim while others stay on the lookout for

crocodiles. Our guide took us on walks around the island, where you learn about the bush and animals, although you can't get as close to them. (See also page 144.)
Contact: www.maun-backpackers.com; Tel +267 686 2406

Plettenberg Bay – elephant experience
The Elephant Sanctuary is a temporary home for young elephants before they are old and independent enough to be released into a suitable environment. Here you can touch, feed and brush the elephants. An elephant ride takes you through the forest and fynbos, where one can envisage the life of the mysterious Knysna elephant that used to roam here.
Contact: www.elephantsanctuary.co.za; Tel 044 534 8145

Victoria Falls – elephant safari
The Wild Horizons Wildlife Sanctuary rehabilitates rescued elephants. Most

of these beasts would no longer survive in the wild and have adapted to living in the sanctuary. Riding on an elephant is comfortable; you practically sit on a big lounge chair. High up, you can view other animals as you walk through the grasslands of the Victoria Falls National Park. (See also page 150.)
Contact: www.wildhorizons.co.za;
Tel +263 013 44571

Kenya – learning about snakes and other reptiles
The sign at the Bio-Ken Snake Farm in Watamu reads: 'Visitors welcome at their own risk'. You'll find a wide variety of snakes from around the world, including rattlesnakes. The guides explain the different species and their dangers. Bio-Ken principally functions as a laboratory, research centre and producer of bio-toxins. It is also home to tortoises, lizards, crocodiles and frogs.

You are very safe, as all the snakes are in tanks and snake handlers have to know what they are doing, especially when they milk the snakes of their venom.
Contact: www.bio-ken.com; Tel +254 718 290 324

Plettenberg Bay – snake handling
Lawnwood Snake Sanctuary is a great controlled environment to learn how to handle non-venomous snakes. The smaller snakes seem to be more agile and wriggly, and tend to slither away, whereas the bigger constrictors, like the African rock python, move more sluggishly and make you feel more at ease with their slow, graceful movements. The snake handlers enter the pits containing venomous snakes like puff adders – which proves that snakes won't attack you if they don't feel threatened. The really dangerous mambas, cobras and vipers are in tanks where you can study their appearance and thereby hopefully recognise them in the wild.
Contact: 044 534 8056

SNOW & ICE

Even though we live in the southern hemisphere, snow gives me the feeling of Christmas. The festive atmosphere is the same in July – cosy dinners with Glühwein, snowball fights and high-activity days packed with fun. Global warming seems to have the opposite effect on us down south, with increasing snowfall every year.

WINTER KIT

Outdoor activities in winter do not have to be something to dread. With the right threads, it's liberating to be out in the elements and feel comfortable. Each winter sport has its own special kit, but these items are a must for winter activities:

- Thermal underwear – a base layer that traps the air and creates heat, and keeps your skin dry.
- Middle layer – fleece tops are great insulators combined with the base layer.
- Shell jacket – protects from wind and rain.
- Down jacket – this is the first thing I pack in winter. It's incredibly warm and regulates your body temperature. Often it's warm enough with just a base layer.
- Woollen socks – make a big difference, especially if you wear them under leather boots, which provide a layer of protection and insulation.
- Gloves – various thicknesses are available according to the cold and the degree of manoeuvrability you

require. Mitts are often the warmest option, as they create more body heat, but allow less manoeuvrability.
- Beanie – they say you lose most of your body heat through your head. Keeping your ears and head covered with a woollen beanie goes a long way to diminish heat loss.
- Sunscreen – it may not be the first thing you think about, but winter sunburn can be nasty. The sun reflects off the snow, which gives you double exposure to the rays.

Places we recommend
Lesotho – AfriSki

An amphitheatre-shaped feature 3 000 metres up in the Maluti Mountains, along the Moteng Pass, is home to the AfriSki resort. In winter there is enough snowfall, combined with a state-of-the-art snow-making system, to provide good skiing conditions on the kilometre-long ski slope, serviced by a T-bar lift. There is also a shorter intermediate and beginner slope, a world-class freestyle snow park, and a bum-board alley for kids and adults. With the ski or snowboard

school, shop and après-ski bar, it is everything like a European ski holiday, although on a much smaller scale.

The vibe is festive and continues long into the night. This is Africa, so the snowy season only lasts from June to August. After good snowfall, tracks appear all over the mountain as skiers and snowboarders go off piste to ride the powder snow that everyone loves. (See also page 152.)
Contact: www.afriski.net;
Tel 0861AFRISKI (0861 237 4754);
and www.goneskiing.com; Tel 0861 754 669

Drakensberg – Giant's Castle
The experience of climbing vertical ice is something not easily explained in South Africa. To climb on ice requires skill and special ice tools. Once you trust your gear, there's a sense of power as your pointy crampons and sharp ice axes find purchase in the hard ice, which allows you to ascend the frozen waterfalls. Every year, at the height of winter, the gullies and amphitheatre at Giant's Castle freeze, allowing us to ice climb. This is as close to Alpine climbing as it gets in South Africa and it is a great training ground if you are planning a trip to the Alps. The walk is long, steep and cold. There are many ice features here from 30 to 200 metres in height, and of various degrees of difficulty.

The quality and quantity of ice change every year with the seasonal rainfall and temperatures, so you'll never climb the same feature twice. This is a remote area with shepherds roaming the land, and although they're harmless, it is recommended not to leave gear unguarded.

Various sections of the Mountain Club of South Africa meet here every year and are always happy to take beginners.
Contact: www.mcsa.org.za

ADRENALIN: BUNGEE JUMPING & ZIP LINING (CANOPY TOURS)

Adrenalin is a hormone released during high stress or exciting situations. Some people say they're addicted to it and this has created a market for certain activities. I associate the feeling with fear, and I'm not sure it's something I want to be addicted to.

Bungee jumping and king swing both entail you leaping off a platform into space. With a bungee, you bounce on the elastic string, facing down, until the operator either pulls you back up or lowers you down. The king swing makes more sense to me – a static rope is attached to your waist harness and your jump is initially like a free fall until the rope catches (it is attached to a structure opposite) and creates a pendulum swing in the air while you stay upright.

Canopy tours have taken the old fufi slide to the next level. You glide along a steel cable high up in the treetops, over gorges and waterfalls, which can be exhilarating.

Places to bungee jump and king swing
Bloukrans Bridge
The Bloukrans Bungee is known as the world's highest commercial bungee jump – 216 metres above the Bloukrans River. Friends can join you on a safe, yet exposed, walkway under the bridge to the arch, where you have a great view of people leaping into space. It is also one of the most beautiful parts of the country and you can see the mouth of the river as it flows into the sea.
Contact: www.faceadrenalin.com; Tel 042 281 1458 or 071 248 5959

Vic Falls
Jumping 111 metres into air with a cord around your ankles is more than a thrill. Personally, I think the scenery is irrelevant at that point, but if you do need a reason to choose this bungee, it would be the roaring white water rushing below the great Victoria Falls – the largest sheet of falling water in the world.

The bridge swing has the same rush but allows you to swing over the water instead of bouncing upside down. The bridge slide is a zip line across the gorge from Zimbabwe to Zambia – a mild and fun ride for the less daring.
Contact: www.victoriafallsbungee.com; Tel +260 213 324 231

Soweto

The Orlando Towers, decorated with murals depicting Soweto's history, are a bright landmark in the urban landscape. At 100 metres, the two towers are lower than most of the commercial bungee bridges but no less intimidating to jump from. You also have the option of either the bungee jump (straight down) or the power swing (straight down, followed by a long swing). There are many other activities based at the towers catering for different degrees of fearlessness.
Contact: www.orlandotowers.co.za; Tel 071 674 4343

Durban

The king swing from near the top of the Moses Mabhida Stadium over its pitch is awesome, if you like adrenalin. You also get a chance to ride in the Sky Car, walk over the arch and on the pitch.
Contact: www.bigrush.co.za; Tel 031 312 9435

Places to do canopy tours
Tsitsikamma

The Tsitsikamma Canopy Tour was the first to be established in South Africa and it's easy to see why. The ancient tall trees of this indigenous forest are among the natural attractions of this area and canopy gliding gives you a chance to view them from close up. (See also page 100.)
Contact: www.canopytour.co.za; Tel 042 535 0150

Storms River

This is an easy-access zip line eight kilometres from the Storms River Bridge, on the N2. The slides follow the Kruis River over waterfalls. There are eight slides all close to one another, so it doesn't take too long and can be conveniently fitted into your travel arrangements. The longest slide is 211 metres. (See also page 91.)
Contact: www.ziplinetour.co.za; Tel 072 141 1804

Karkloof

Most of the Karkloof Canopy Tour is in the thick indigenous forest of the area. The highest platform is 30 metres, and the longest slide is 180 metres, giving you the sensation of flying through the trees. If you have a fear of heights, you may not

enjoy this. The almost-tropical sound of birds and monkeys adds to the experience. (See also page 62.)
Contact: www.karkloofcanopytour.co.za;
Tel 033 330 3415

Magaliesberg

Black eagles can be spotted in this area as you glide 30 metres above ground down the Ysterkloof Gorge. There are 11 platforms with simple take-offs. The first glide is at a gentle angle, and they get steeper as you progress down the gorge, but are never unduly scary. It is an effortless way to discover nature around you on a different level. (See also page 12.)
Contact: www.magaliescanopytour.co.za;
Tel 014 535 0150 or 079 492 0467

Magoebaskloof

The George's Valley Gorge offers a bird's-eye view of the dazzling waterfalls and rapids in the Groot Letaba River. The longest of the 11 lines is 140 metres, and it's easy to slow down and stop during the slides while you look down a waterfall or a deep pool. It's a beautiful and safe experience.
Contact: www.magoebaskloofcanopytour.co.za;
Tel 083 866 1546

BIG AIR: PARAGLIDING, SKYDIVING, TANDEM GLIDING & HOT-AIR BALLOONING

'Once you have tasted flight, you will forever walk the earth with your eyes turned skyward, for there you have been, and there you will always long to return.' – Leonardo Da Vinci

Every person has a different attitude to heights and flying. Of all the 'big air' sports, I find microlighting the most tame. Just because you're not falling at high velocity doesn't mean that paragliding is not exhilarating. The fact that you can go up and down, along cliff faces at high speed and dwell above the clouds allows you the time to acknowledge your fear and excitement. If you're prone to motion sickness, my advice is to fly on a day that is calm and predictable. There is no drug or device that will prevent nausea in turbulent conditions.

When you skydive, your adrenalin level is so high you won't have time to feel sick. I remember my surprise at the control and clarity of every feeling during free fall – a feeling I wish everyone could experience.

Gliding in a plane without an engine, where the height you achieve and distance you cover are attained through sheer skill and the elements, gives you a great understanding of how birds fly.

PARAGLIDING

If you are not a qualified pilot, you can sign up for a tandem flight where all you do is sit back and enjoy the view. If the bug bites, you can join a paragliding school and learn to fly yourself. You need to be 16 years old to get your licence, but one can do a tandem flight at any age, provided you are big enough to fit into the harness.

Drakensberg

The Drakensberg has another perspective to its beauty that not everyone gets to see – from the clouds. In the south, you can fly from Bulwer, where there is a permanent flying school, and discover the lay of the land. To the north, you can enquire at the Champagne Castle Hotel about tandem pilots who will take you for a flip.

At the launch areas, you run down a steep hill in tandem until your feet gently lift off the ground and the valleys below become smaller and smaller as you climb the thermals. Generally, you stay on the fringes of the Berg, as flying is not permitted over national heritage sites.

You can find a tandem pilot by contacting the South African Hang Gliding and Paragliding Association www.sahpa.co.za.

Dunnottar Winch Park

The mine dumps of the East Rand are not particularly scenic, but if you want a quick fix of flying fever, this is an easy day out from Joburg and there are calm thermals rising over the flat land. You are 'winched' into the air by a cord attached to a car until you're high enough to catch the thermals. You can have paragliding lessons here; and it is also a great location if you just want to try a paragliding session with a tandem pilot.

Contact: www.sahpa.co.za

Bambi, Mpumalanga

This is another great site for either learning or for people who just want to go for a flip. The launch and landing spots are ideal, and the thermals released from the valley almost guarantee good flying.

Various clubs fly from here, and you can find a pilot or trainer at www.sahpa.co.za

Cape Town

On those beautiful summer days in Cape Town, one often sees paragliders soaring around Lion's Head and over the beaches. It is fascinating to observe the extraordinary topography of this city from above. With a paraglider, you get to do so in silence while you feel the breeze and fresh air.

Contact: www.birdmen.co.za; Tel 021 557 8144 or 082 658 6710

Porterville

Once you have a pilot's licence, you can fly in one of the ultimate flying sites in the world. Porterville, in the Cederberg, is known for its great cross-country flying thermals, which allow you to stay up for long periods along the ridge and around the Groot Winterhoek Mountains. The area has a couple of launch sites, which makes the activity accessible. (See also page 108.)

Contact: www.flyporterville.info; Tel 022 931 3567

Sedgefield and Wilderness

This part of the coast is a popular place for retirement but you're never too old for adventure. The paragliding spots are easy to get to and the conditions mild, which make this area a great place for learning, and a beautiful setting for anyone, any age, to fly and get a unique perspective on this coastal hideaway with its fynbos-covered dunes and extensive lakes. (See also page 102.)

Contact: www.cloudbase-paragliding.co.za; Tel 044 877 1414

HOT-AIR BALLOONING

Ballooning is extravagantly enjoyable, and seems to belong to the realm of fantasy animation films.

Paarl

Floating through blue skies, past soft clouds, over the wine region of Paarl in the early-morning soft light is almost unreal, but not impossibly out of reach with wineland ballooning.

Contact: www.kapinfo.com; Tel 021 863 3192 or 083 983 4687

GLIDING

Flying in a two-seater glider is a peaceful way to take to the skies, with only the sound of the air as you circle up in the thermals. Birds are a good indication of where to find the hot rising air. Gliders do not rely on engines and gracefully share this space in peace with the birds. The best gliding season is between October and April.

Gariep Dam

The Gariep Dam is well known for gliding, and world records have been made here. You fly over the vast dam and the surrounding tawny countryside or up the bends of the Orange River. (See also page 82.)
Contact: www.gariepdamaviation.com

SKYDIVING

My nerves always build up while sitting in the plane, waiting to reach altitude. Once the dive master opens the door, you know there's no other way out and somehow everything becomes automatic. Unlike bungee jumps, with skydiving you fall for long enough to compose yourself and enjoy the feeling of free flight. This is the best part, especially when you realise you're in control. The feeling is the same for tandem and solo flights.

Carletonville

The mine dumps of Carletonville aren't a place where you would normally consider spending your weekends, but it's a buzzing hub of adrenalin junkies from Gauteng. A qualified tandem instructor, and their camera crew, will take any keen non-

skydiver for a flip to taste the wild side. (See also page 16.)
Contact: www.skydivejoburg.co.za; Tel 084 998 3178

Okavango Delta by air

The Okavango Delta is so big that the only way to comprehend the layout and size of it is to take a scenic flight, preferably at sunset when all the animals are near the waterholes. The landscape looks like a giant puzzle with numerous veins of water splitting the land. (See also page 144).
Contact: www.mackair.co.bw; Tel +267 686 0675

URBAN ADVENTURES

Most of us have become habitual creatures of the urban jungle and many of us need to shrug this off by taking part in adventures over weekends and holidays. You may not realise it, but our cities have a lot to offer to keep you psyched and keen on life.

The following is a summary of some urban adventures available in South Africa's major cities.

ARCHERY
Joburg

Archery is more than a competitive sport – it is an ancient art that was practised by the Egyptians thousands of years ago. The thrill of watching the arrow take off in the right direction and thud into the target is similar to that of a fishing line when you get the casting right and the movement feels effortless. Technique is important as you transfer energy from your body to the arrow. Beginners, and advanced courses are offered at the Mark's Park Sports club. Contact: www.sanaa.org.za; Tel 011 559 2416

MOTOR RACING
Pretoria

The whine of racing cars is a good indication that you are getting close to the Zwartkops Raceway, west of Pretoria. Motor racing is expensive and inaccessible to most of us, but anyone can sign up for the Driver Training Centre here and up their driving skills. The club also has a race every month. Although this is not a physical activity, it certainly involves adrenalin and focus. Contact: www.zwartkops.co.za; Tel 012 384 2291

ROLLERBLADING
Durban

Durban's promenade buzzes in the late afternoon along the mile-long stretch of smooth paving between uShaka Marine World and Suncoast Casino, a space shared by runners, walkers, cyclists, skate boarders, rollerbladers and moms with prams. A skate park in the middle includes some features to hone your skills on anything with wheels. It's a place where you are surrounded by fit and active people of all ability levels.

AERIAL SILKS
Joburg

An arty discipline known as aerial silks is gaining popularity in South Africa as a way to stay in shape. It originated in the circus, but now this art form is taking off. Regardless of your fitness level, size or age, you can lift off from the ground, if only for a

few minutes, and feel graceful suspended from two silk bands. Anyone can do what looks unachievable, and it gives you a wonderful feeling of empowerment. Aerial silks impart a flowing motion that makes the poses appear effortless and elegant. It does require some energy and core-muscle strength, and is a great alternative to conventional workouts.
Contact: www.aerialarts.co.za; Tel 011 476 2192

CRITICAL MASS
Joburg, Cape Town, Durban
Critical Mass cycle rides are a celebration of cycling in public spaces, and raise awareness of the need for safe urban cycle paths. Cyclists in Joburg, Cape Town and Durban can join people in more than 300 major cities worldwide, from San Francisco to Tokyo, on the last Friday night of every month. Hundreds of people cycle in a group, which makes it safe while you pass through parts of the city you may never have seen before. There is a good social vibe and the pace is slow, so anyone can join in. (See also page 22.)
Contact: www.criticalmass.co.za

JOZI X
Joburg
The best way to describe Jozi X is a jungle gym for adults – although it also caters for children. This is a place to try out all the tricks you always thought you'd be good at while watching *Gladiators*. The obstacles are surrounded by big inflatable mats, so it is impossible to hurt yourself. It is great fun to compete against your mates and does require some focus. You become aware of how to shift your balance to achieve moves that seem to be impossible at first.
Contact: www.jozix.co.za; Tel 082 456 2358

ACROBRANCH
Joburg
The best way to describe Acrobranch is as a glorified jungle gym – for adults and kids. This concept has taken off in Europe in the form of places to practise balance and unusual movements. Acrobranch is a safe and easy environment that allows you to get used to heights with an escape route at every step. Protective gear is provided.
Contact: www.acrobranch.co.za; Tel 078 438 7463

Text © *Sunday Times* 2013
Photographs © *Sunday Times* 2013

ISBN: 978-1-920434-48-9

First edition, first impression 2013

Published jointly by
Bookstorm (Pty) Limited, PO Box 4532, Northcliff 2115, Johannesburg, South Africa
www.bookstorm.co.za
and
Pan Macmillan South Africa (Pty) Limited, Private Bag X19, Northlands 2116, Johannesburg, South Africa
www.panmacmillan.co.za

Distributed by Pan Macmillan
via Booksite Afrika

Edited by Mark Ronan
Proofread by Wesley Thompson
Photography by Marianne Schwankhart, unless otherwise stated
Cover design by mr design
Book design and typesetting by René de Wet
Printed by Ultra Litho (Pty) Ltd